GILDED AGE COCKTAILS

Gilded Age Cocktails

HISTORY, LORE, AND RECIPES

FROM AMERICA'S GOLDEN AGE

Cecelia Tichi

WASHINGTON MEWS BOOKS

An Imprint of

NEW YORK UNIVERSITY PRESS

New York

WASHINGTON MEWS BOOKS
An Imprint of
NEW YORK UNIVERSITY PRESS
New York
www.nyupress.org

Illustrations by Julia Mills
Book designed and typeset by Charles B. Hames

References to Internet websites (URLs) were accurate at the time of writing.
Neither the author nor New York University Press is responsible for URLs
that may have expired or changed since the manuscript was prepared.

Library of Congress Cataloging-in-Publication Data
Names: Tichi, Cecelia, 1942–   author.
Title: Gilded Age cocktails : history, lore, and recipes from America's golden age /
Cecelia Tichi.
Description: New York : New York University Press, [2020] |
Includes bibliographical references and index.
Identifiers: LCCN 2020029697 (print) | LCCN 2020029698 (ebook) |
ISBN 9781479805259 (cloth) | ISBN 9781479805266 (ebook other) |
ISBN 9781479805280 (ebook)
Subjects: LCSH: Cocktails—United States. | United States—Social life and
customs—1865–1918.
Classification: LCC TX951 .T49 2020 (print) | LCC TX951 (ebook) |
DDC 641.87/4—dc23
LC record available at https://lccn.loc.gov/2020029697
LC ebook record available at https://lccn.loc.gov/2020029698

New York University Press books are printed on acid-free paper, and their binding
materials are chosen for strength and durability. We strive to use environmentally
responsible suppliers and materials to the greatest extent possible in publishing
our books.

Manufactured in the United States of America

Also available as an ebook

CONTENTS

Introduction

"A Gilded Cocktail"

In the decades following the American Civil War, the nation was bursting with innovation—the telephone, the motorcar, electric lights, the airplane, and a host of other marvels. For the newly sophisticated palates eager for novelty at every turn, no invention was more ubiquitous among the affluent than the beverage soon to be heralded as the *cocktail*.

The word "cocktail" might summon thoughts of a rooster's flaring feathers, but the term has no connection to a barnyard cock. It originated in the equestrian practice of distinguishing purebred horses from others whose bloodlines were mixed. The tails of non-Thoroughbred (mongrel) steeds were docked, or cocktailed, to distinguish them on sight from the superior Thoroughbreds. Before the word "cocktails" could head a menu of drinkables for the upper classes, the term needed a makeover, for the idea of a cocktail as something tainted or impure had made its way to the oases where distilled spirits reigned. In the early 1800s, the term "cock-tail" warned against a concoction that "fuddles the head" or was secretly diluted. Let the imbiber beware!

The celebrants of cocktails need also beware the admonitions that trailed drink from colonial times, for America had amassed a thick ledger of dire warnings against alcohol. In 1673, the pamphlet *Wo to Drunkards*, written by the eminent Puritan minister Increase Mather, inveighed against "sinners in Zion," despoilers of the Lord's chosen New World "City upon a Hill." The clergyman, like most colonists, routinely slaked his thirst with beer, for brewing was known to be a hedge against ills from dodgy water, but pleasurable tippling for its own sake was proscribed. Nonetheless, a century later, during the American Revolution, soldiers of the Continental Army under General George Washington received a daily ration of rum that boosted morale and has been credited with reenlistments.

In the public mind, where sober practicality was the bulwark of American progress, the linkage of poetic inspiration with Dionysian revels complicated the issue of sobriety and creativity. Henry Wadsworth Longfellow (b. 1807) lauded hard work in his poem "The Village Blacksmith" (and was forgiven for another verse rhyming "Catawba wine" with "taste more divine"). Nathaniel Hawthorne (b. 1804), for his part, followed his bestselling novels *The Scarlet Letter* and *The House of the Seven Gables* with *The Blithedale Romance* and the pronouncement that "human nature . . . has a naughty instinct that approves of wine . . . if not of stronger liquor." Hawthorne wished a "blight" upon vineyards of the rich, and lamented that the poor sought succor in "the muddy medium of . . . liquor." But the literary ledger was irrevocably stained by the sodden Edgar Allan Poe (b. 1809) and his ilk, whose habits were thought to threaten the moral fiber of the new nation. Upon Poe's death in 1849, the *New York Herald* ran an editorial vilifying this cadre of "weak and helpless" American writers, a vain and conceited lot, bereft of "common sense—the basis of all usefulness and success in life." "As a class," fumed the newspaper, "they naturally take to the bottle."

By the later 1800s, the stuffy Victorian era had ebbed, finally, to herald the decades welcoming the cocktail. Queen Victoria's son Prince Edward VII endowed the period with his name, and "Edwardian" became synonymous with the age of the bon vivant. Across the channel, France celebrated the Belle Epoque, and in the US, a young writer dubbing himself Mark Twain collaborated in 1873 with Charles Dudley Warner on a novel that defined the era: *The Gilded Age*. In the book, we see traveling businessmen carrying "brandy flasks" en route to a saloon. "Gentlemen," advises the leader of the group, "never take an inferior liquor."

For imbibing celebrants, the Gilded Age might also be known as the Golden Age of Cocktails. During the period from the 1870s to the 1910s, as rapid industrialization led to the accumulation of staggering wealth for the very few, then as now the doings of the rich and famous cast a long shadow on social tastes. While immigrants and workers had their own drinking patterns, the expanding census of affluent Americans took a lesson from the very rich, and coast to coast the mixed drink flourished at dinner parties and sporting events, luncheons and balls, on ocean liners and yachts, in barrooms, summer resorts, and hotels. The drinks ranged from mild concoctions such as the Florida cocktail, which combined iced orange juice and sweet Italian vermouth, to the potent signature brew of the copper mining regions of Montana, which called for port wine, brandy, and French vermouth. The designated "cocktail hour" of the Gilded Age varied according to desire or necessity. It might begin early in the day, when under the influence of the "hangover" one needed the "hair

of the dog that bit" the preceding night, and continue un-
abated until, at last, the bottles were corked and set aside—
ready for the following day.

Exactly how a cooled whiskey or gin drink began to inau-
gurate the cocktail era may never be known, but the fact is the
engine of the new cocktail era was, quite simply, ice, which
had been profitably harvested from US frozen lakes and rivers
since the 1820s. Cut and warehoused in "ice houses," the wintry "crop" was an indispensable coolant for perishable com-
modities shipped great distances by sea and rail. By the later
1800s, mechanization modernized ice production, and Mark
Twain marveled that every Mississippi River town, including
New Orleans, "has her ice factory" producing "big blocks" of
ice, all "crystal clear."

Whether in New Orleans, New York, Chicago, San Francisco, Virginia City, Nevada, or elsewhere, someone found
that a whiskey drink cooled with ice chips or cubes that chimed
against the glass was not tainted, but pleasing and preferred.
The social seigneur of Gilded Age etiquette, the Savannah-
born Ward McAllister (b. 1827), sounds like a latter-day wine
snob in his stuffy memoir, *Society as I Have Found It*, but his recipe
for the champagne frappé, with its "little flakes of ice," bowed
to the possibilities of the cocktail.

If ice improved the experience, perhaps further enhance-
ments lay ahead, and why not? Patrons "in their cups" soon
lifted crystal stemware, glass tumblers, and stout barware filled
with cocktails named for notable persons and places in their
circuit. Dispensed in a stirrup cup on Kentucky Derby Day or
ladled from a silver bowl on the first morning of the New Year,
the julep and the "spiked" punch (and numerous kindred libations) marked the calendar for year-round celebration.

The flavorings and fruits in cocktails often hinted of the tropics or other exotic locales far from the mahogany bars where drinks were served. Bartenders and patrons owed much to the busy depots, coastal ports, and cargo ships that hummed with activity during the Gilded Age. In economic terms, overbuilt railroads brought on financial crises in the 1870s and 1890s, but the expansive rail network expedited shipments of oranges, lemons, and limes from Southern California and Florida to the cocktail bars in the wintry cities of the North. The docks of San Francisco and Los Angeles welcomed pineapples and sugar from Hawaii, and stevedores at work on East Coast ports unloaded bounteous fruit from the Caribbean. International shipping, what's more, brought whiskeys and liqueurs from Scotland, Ireland, and the Continent. While the snow fell and icicles dangled outdoors, an Orange Blossom or a Santiago cocktail transported the imbiber to sunny, warm, distant climes.

The "iron horse" played another part in the rise of the cocktail. A half-century prior to the Gilded Age, the French traveler Alexis De Tocqueville had noted Americans' mastery of "the art of joining." A network of railroads now propelled a gregarious country into the busy industrial era of steam and steel. Annually, rail lines sped business groups and conventioneers from far-flung locales to central US cities for fellowship, for deals—and for drinks. A veteran bartender observed that "some men will drink . . . to show their diamonds and jewelry, their fancy clothes, and mainly their money," but "most men will drink because it is 'business.'"

A trove of souvenir menus from business and professional conventions across the country tells the tale. Medical societies and journalists imbibed as they gathered, as did athletic clubs, chambers of commerce, and reunions of military regiments. A head-spinning roster of imbibing cohorts included piano dealers, telegraphers, customs inspectors, bankers, carriage builders, pawn brokers, grocers, paper box manufacturers, postmasters, telegraphers, and countless others. The fraternal lodges (Elks, Moose, Lions, Masons) assembled, as did the Merchant Tailor's National Protective Association of America, the Knights of Revelry, the salesforce of the Hildreth Tarnish Company, and the Washington University class of 1896.

For those who were used to drinking their whiskey straight, an "educated thirst" required schooling and the syllabus could be a challenge. Just as novice museumgoers learned to "touch" paintings and sculptures with their eyes instead of their hands, so the cocktail bar required on-site tutorials. George Boldt (b. 1851), manager of New York's Waldorf, tried in vain to help patrons distinguish between liquors and liqueurs. Visitors from the "hinterlands" especially objected to brandy served in "glasses the size of thimbles"; as one legendarily brayed, "I am a he-man, I am, and when I drink liquor, I want plenty of it. Bring the bottle and a tall glass!" Refusing to see why "a fine old Napoleon, 1804, or Chartreuse or

Benedictine" was to be sipped, not gulped, these customers eventually concocted highballs of the liqueurs, diluting the spirits with a quantity of ice and soda or other mixer, to the benefit of the proprietor's "exchequer" and the dismay of the manager.

Like hard liquor, the cocktail was a masculine preserve until quite late in the Gilded Age, probably because a battery of strict etiquette books gave ladies no permission to consume such drinks. While ladies might routinely enjoy champagne and wines over several courses at a dinner party, and liqueurs and cigarettes at the conclusion of the meal, before the turn of the twentieth century no lady "bellied up to the bar," raised her delicate calfskin boot to the brass rail below, and ordered a drink. When Boldt installed small cocktail tables and chairs in lieu of a bar in the Waldorf Hotel, the notion of ladies and gentlemen imbibing together at the cocktail hour might have flickered across his mind before he banished the scandalous thought and bowed to social convention, naming the new locale the Men's Café.

Cocktails honoring men's colleges and universities had no counterparts in the women's colleges. In public places, a young lady was expected to request Appolinaris, the "Queen of Table Waters" (named for the patron saint of wine!). The young ladies of the "Seven Sisters" colleges enjoyed teatimes, but if any of them dared to nip from a young man's silver flask at an outdoor sporting event they were mum on the practice. A few glimmers, however, suggest that cocktails were not altogether alien beverages for ladies, but served in private or in disguise. Around Madison Square, according to one chronicler of New York customs, "a famous confectionary store" provided cocktails to those "who knew the ropes." The drinks, "brought from the bar of an adjacent hotel . . . were served in tea-cups." (The high alcoholic content of women's "medicinal" products was legendary.)

Private weekend house parties became the prime venue for mixed drinks in mixed company. Financier Pembroke Jones (b. 1858) and his wife, Sarah, were "famous" for the "high balls and mint Julips" served at their coastal home in Wilmington, North Carolina. After "several cocktails," confessed social arbiter Henry Lehr (b. 1869), "I became strongly gay." In New York, Colonel William d'Alton Mann (b. 1839), editor and publisher of the notorious Gilded Age scandal sheet *Town Topics*, hosted celebrated weekend parties from April to November at his country house upstate at Lake George. For the editors and their wives or girlfriends, who departed Grand Central Thursday afternoon on a reserved Pullman car for a weekend of outdoor festivities, the day began with Scotch and Sodas at breakfast. Thereafter, at the colonel's summons on the half-hour ("Say, ducks, ain't you dry?"), continuous cocktails were mixed and served by the colonel's daughter, Emma. One must imagine her plying the cocktail shaker, the swizzle stick, the siphon, the crystal-clear ice, an array of polished glasses, and bottled elixirs without limit, a true mistress of the bar.

Ironically, the same technologies that supplied alcoholic spirits to Gilded Age imbibers emboldened their enemies. Newspapers that advertised new inventories of liquors, wines, and ale also provided outlets for the opinions and agitation of the proponents of temperance. The railroads that brought spirits and their consumers together also transported pro-Prohibition folks to meetings where beliefs hardened into strategies for public support and legislative action. Echoing

the colonial denunciations of the "devil's brew," the Women's Christian Temperance Society (WTCU) and the Anti-Saloon League mounted parallel campaigns, and politically powerful clergy joined the fight against the spirits blamed for wrecking the lives of individuals and entire families. The partisan split dividing the imbibing "wets" from the teetotaling "drys" widened, shaming convivial tipplers as sots bent on destroying the sanctity of the American home.

In January 1920, the Eighteenth Amendment to the Constitution, banning the "manufacture, sale, or transportation of intoxicating liquors," became the law of the land (until it was itself repealed by another constitutional amendment thirteen years later). The heyday of the sparkling glass of the Gilded Age was over and the era of "speakeasies," "rum running," and the "roaring twenties" had begun, heralding another chapter in the evolution of the cocktail.

AUTHOR'S NOTE

Although numerous guides to the Golden Age of Cocktails were produced by the era's celebrated mixologists, a particularly invaluable forerunner must be singled out here: Albert S. Crockett's *The Old Waldorf-Astoria Bar Book* (1931, 1934) is a veritable atlas of pre-Prohibition cocktails by name and ingredients. Though Crockett's Klondike and Hawaii cocktails call for identical ingredients (and may be something of a geographic joke), the richness of Crockett's *Peacocks on Parade*, his memoir of the Gilded Age, gives one confidence in the accuracy of the *Bar* book. Many of the drinks he chronicles have drifted away, but a few familiar names endure to this day, with ingredients long since adapted to modern tastes. Crockett's historic recipes, including the Manhattan and Martini cocktails, indicate that Gilded Age imbibers both quenched their thirst and satisfied a "sweet tooth."

A social observer of the Gilded Age, Crockett lived through those years and, like others of the era, wrote its story at first hand. His dictionary of drinks is foundational here, and his "Glossary" flavors these pages.

1

Olympians of the Bar

"One more round, if you please . . . I'll have another."

While a fair location and standard stock of whiskies and kegs might guarantee a bar's modest success, during the Gilded Age a Svengali of cocktails raised the oasis of alcoholic drinks to new Himalayan heights. As requests and plaudits rained, gifted mixologists soloed behind mahogany countertops, their movements as deft as the nimblest jugglers, precise as laboratory chemists, efficient as well-calibrated time-pieces, and intuitive as psychologists who assessed their clients' deepest needs and desires. Cocktail "engineering" elevated these inventors to the stratosphere of libations and each "majestic figure," swathed in his white apron, could be a candidate for a hall of fame for Gilded Age men of the bar. Such honorees might include John F. Peterson, principal bartender of Kirk & Co.'s bar on lower Broadway, synonymous with "bibulous respectability," whose "resplendent bald head" was "a beacon" guiding patrons to his bar; Charley Sander of the Tall Tower in the basement of the *Tribune* at the corner of Spruce and Nassau, the site of the original Tammany Hall, "whose moustache compared with any of the day with its tip-top measurement"; Charley McCarty, who "presided with dignity and efficiency" over the barroom of the St. James Hotel at Broadway and Twenty-Sixth; and Billy Patterson, who claimed "that he could win the lasting friendship of any man if he were but permitted to mix him a drink."

But the true Paul Bunyan of the bar, and its peripatetic maestro, was indisputably Jerry Thomas. Born in 1830 in New Haven, Connecticut, to parents who hoped their son would be called to the ministry, Jerry would eventually find his pulpit behind the bar, dispensing his inventive delectations across numerous states of the Union and abroad. The restless Thomas apprenticed in saloons from New Orleans to San Francisco, honed his craft at Planters' House in St. Louis and the silver mining boomtown of Nevada's Virginia City, and poured libations as far away as London. He even served a stint at a New York bar near P. T. Barnum's museum, which had featured Tom Thumb and a strutting "Hercules" in a Yankee Doodle suit.

Thomas won early fame for his Blue Blazer, a pyrotechnic dazzler he developed while bartending at the El Dorado Saloon in the San Francisco gold rush days. "On a bitter night," writes one chronicler, a customer arrived "fresh from the isolation of the gold fields" to demand that Thomas serve him "the flames of hell in liquid form 'that'll shake me right down to the gizzard.'" For persuasive purposes, the customer wore pistols, "with which to enforce his extravagant demands."

Thomas gave "due consideration" to this "chemical" problem, then gathered two silver mugs, scotch whisky, boiling water, sugar, a lemon peel, and went to work. According to one witness, "there was a hush as the piping liquid sizzled down the long-parched throat." The drink left the gold miner "awestruck," and "with what voice he could muster, the fellow assured Professor Thomas that his gizzard had, indeed, been shaken." The signature beverage:

BLUE BLAZER

Ingredients

> 2 hot silver mugs (with insulated handles)
>
> 1 or 2 ounces scotch whisky
>
> 4 ounces boiling water
>
> 2 lumps sugar
>
> Lemon peel

Directions

> 1. Pour scotch into first mug.
> 2. Pour water and sugar into second mug.
> 3. Set scotch alight and allow to burn for about 2 minutes while pouring it into second mug.
> 4. Quickly pour lighted mixture back and forth from mug to mug.
> 5. When fire is extinguished, serve in one of the mugs with lemon peel. (Additional whisky can be added.)

Thomas eventually assumed a posting as principal bartender at New York's Metropolitan Hotel at Prince Street and Broadway, "in the days when the metropolis was the scene of the soundest drinking on earth," where he set a diamond-studded standard. Diamonds were a necessity for "the presentation of self" in Gilded Age New York, and the man behind the bar owed his customers and himself a glittering array from cuffs to collar. Called "public jewels," diamonds were "meant to be noticed, gaped at, admired, and desired," and mandatory for "anyone who played a part on the urban stage." Jerry Thomas glittered as he worked, "all ablaze with diamonds," including "gorgeous diamond rings" flashing on his fingers.

Gilded Age manuals abounded with how-to-advice for every conceivable occupation, from clerk to cook, prizefighter to engineer, and with his encyclopedic knowledge Thomas promised to introduce Americans to the sophisticated libations known throughout Britain, Europe, and Russia. His first *Bar-tender's Guide*, published in 1862, offered ten straightforwardly named cocktails: Bottle, Brandy, Fancy Brandy, Whiskey, Champagne, Gin, Fancy Gin, Japanese, Soda, and Jersey. An expanded 1877 edition—*The Bon-Vivant's Companion*—became a much-sought directory of Gilded Age libations. Its menu of 130 drinks ("in endless variety") included the Locomotive, the Balaklava Nector, the Spread Eagle, and numerous encyclopedic listings for every taste and mood. Thomas's "Manual for Manufacture" gave America its modern cocktail menu and made the nation's bartenders lifelong grateful acolytes of the "Professor."

Thomas's signature New York cocktail was a playful twist on his name:

TOM AND JERRY

Ingredients

1 ounce brandy

½ ounce rum

½ egg yolk

1 cup whole milk

Nutmeg

Directions

1. Warm milk and add egg yolk.

2. Add milk and yolk to warmed cup or mug.

3. Add brandy and rum.

4. Stir, dust with grated nutmeg, and serve.

Another renowned bartender, Johnny Solon (or Solan) of New York's Waldorf-Astoria, was celebrated for exquisite improvisation, an unmatched ability to invent a pleasing brand-new cocktail on the spot. Though few soloists of the shaker and swizzle stick have recounted the tales of their exploits, Johnny Solon's invention of the Bronx cocktail was detailed by Albert Steven Crockett (b. 1873), who claims that he heard the story from Solon and recorded it verbatim in his classic *Old Waldorf-Astoria Bar Book*.

Solon was mixing a popular cocktail, the Duplex, when a head waiter at the hotel leaned across the bar and issued a challenge:

"Why don't you get up a new cocktail?" asked the tempter in the tones of a dare. "I have a customer who says you can't do it."

"Can't I?" replied Solon, who finished the Duplex and prepared to meet the challenge, starting with "the equivalent of two jiggers of Gordon Gin" poured into a mixing glass. He then filled "the jigger with orange juice so it made one-third orange juice and two-thirds of gin." He added a dash each of Italian and French vermouths and shook the "thing" up.

Solon swore he did not taste the result, but immediately "poured it into a cocktail glass and handed it" to his challenger, who downed the drink "whole." "By God! You've really got something new!" he exclaimed, "A big hit." "The demand

started that day," recalled Solon. "Pretty soon we were using a whole case of oranges a day. And then several cases."

What to call the new libation? It happened that Johnny Solon had recently visited the Bronx Zoological Park, which had opened in 1899, and the park was on his mind as he mixed the experimental new drink—voilà, the Bronx was created. The cocktail lived on, featured on the drink menus and wine lists at other hotels, such as Boston's Copley-Plaza and Manhattan's Albemarle Hoffman. Variations of the Bronx appeared by and by, but the following recipe hews to Johnny Solon's own recollection. (The ice is presumed.)

THE DUPLEX

Ingredients

1½ ounces French vermouth

1½ ounces Italian vermouth

Orange peel or orange bitters

Directions

1. Combine vermouths in glass with ice.

2. Add squeezed orange peel or bitters.

3. Stir and serve.

THE BRONX (ORIGINAL)

Ingredients

2 parts gin

1 part orange juice

1 dash French vermouth

1 dash Italian vermouth

Ice cubes

Directions

1. Add 2–3 ice cubes to shaker.

2. Add gin and orange juice to shaker.

3. Add dashes of vermouth.

4. Shake, strain, and serve.

Had Johnny Solon guessed that his Bronx cocktail would be a smash hit, he might have considered naming it for himself, as did the mixologist who devised another classic cocktail of the age. The formula for the Gin Fizz concocted in the 1880s by Henry C. Ramos at Meyer's Hotel Internationale restaurant in New Orleans was as mysterious as it was pleasing, for Ramos was loath to reveal his secret. When word spread, customers clamored for the famous fizzes. By 1900, the *Kansas City Star* proclaimed that "Ramos serves a gin fizz that is not equaled anywhere." He later moved on to the Imperial Cabinet Saloon, where Mardi Gras revelers saw dozens of hired "shaker boys" behind the bar, flexing their biceps in service to the master bartender's Gin Fizz.

RAMOS GIN FIZZ

Ingredients

1½ ounces gin

½ ounce simple syrup

1 dash orange flower water

1 egg white

⅓ ounce lemon juice

2 ounces light cream

Directions

1. Fill shaker midway with ice cubes.

2. Add gin and other ingredients.

3. Shake thoroughly (2 minutes).

4. Strain and serve.

The author of another landmark guide, A. William Schmidt, a German immigrant who worked in Chicago's Tivoli Garden before arriving in New York in 1884, was working out of a rundown bar next to the Brooklyn Bridge when he was discovered by a reporter from the *New York Sun*. His cocktails, often crafted of upward of ten ingredients, commanded five dollars apiece (the equivalent of about $130 today) when others were charging fifteen cents, and his recipes for novel drinks for holidays and special occasions were printed in newspapers around the world. For Christmas Eve 1900, his Kaiser's Dream and Siesta were headlined as "Some Wondrous New XMAS Drinks" in Joseph Pulitzer's New York *World*.

Schmidt's 1891 compendium *The Flowing Bowl: When and What to Drink*, attributed to "The Only William," offered sage advice on water, tea, coffee—and milk, "one of the healthiest, most nutritive, and very digestive of beverages." But with "Full Instructions on How to Prepare, Mix, and Serve Beverages," his compendium flowed with wine, beer, spirits, and all pertinent compounds, including some fifty cocktails. With this manual for aspirant bartenders, the author proffered his motto: "True happiness is gained by making others happy." "A man in my profession should never forget that he is a gentleman," Schmidt insisted. "However well-mixed a drink is, much of the flavor will be lost unless politeness is added. A true artist should infuse courtesy and quality into all his liquid pictures." His advice and counsel:

1. As an appropriate suit behind the bar, I would recommend the following: a pair of black trousers, a long, white apron, a white shirt, a white collar, a black tie, a white

vest, and a white coat; care should be taken to have the suit fit well; have the sleeves of your coat cut, that you may button it tight; this will prevent its getting soiled and worn out; never have your suit starched.

2. Clean the top of your counter first, remove all utensils from under the counter and place them on top; clean your bench.

3. Fill all your liquor bottles . . . cut up the fruit for immediate use, clean your silverware.

4. Never allow yourself to be idle behind the bar.

5. A bottle never must be more than half empty.

6. In serving a strained drink, you begin by serving a glass of ice water.

7. For strong drinks, always serve two glasses—one for the drink, the other for the water.

8. When you are not pushed for time, while you are making mixed drinks, cool your glasses with ice before you serve your drink.

9. You may place your glasses together in the form of a pyramid and ornament your structure with fruits and flowers.

10. When a drink is made with ice and then strained, there should be nothing left in the glass but the liquid; the fruit would hinder you in drinking, it would touch the moustache; if you want to eat it, you can't get it out.

11. When you have a drink in which the ice is to remain, in this case use plenty of fruits, as it is pleasing to the eye and allows your guest to eat it if he likes.

12. Shake your drink well; without that you will never get a first-class drink. Good mixing is hard work; but without mixing you spoil the best liquor.

13. For shaking drinks with the shaker, use only a mixing-tumbler; by using goblets you will soil your clothes, and the goblets might break.

14. *Glassware*: In selecting your glassware, choose perfectly white color, also for your bottles, as they look much more inviting. To keep them clean, use egg-shells, salt, paper, or chopped ice.

15. *Fruits*: *Lemons* intended for squeezing should be peeled before using. The juice ought not to be older than a day. . . . The fresh lemon peel is very useful for flavoring and decorating the drinks.

Oranges—a medium size of dark colored ones is the best for squeezing, as well as cutting up. Use from six to twelve oranges, according to the demand of the business.

The Delicious Pineapple—Pineapple may be used in the same way as oranges, the juice or syrup being always indispensable.

Choice Grapes—To make a drink of inviting appearance, choice grapes are necessary, for decorating as well as simply presenting.

In addition to these fruits, a few others ought to be kept on hand: Strawberries, raspberries, blackberries, and cherries. They may be prepared the same way as the other fruits.

Never handle fruits with your fingers, but use a fancy fruit-fork.

As the cocktail craze took hold, those removed from the centers of sophistication could turn, as in most things, to the catalogue of Sears Roebuck & Co. America's retail revolution had begun in 1893, when the Midwestern businessmen Richard Warren Sears and Alvah Curtis Roebuck tapped the US Post Office's new Rural Free Delivery system to launch an annual mail-order catalogue that offered hardware, clothing, sporting goods, jewelry, furniture, and a host of other consumer products to any home in the country, no matter how distant. The Book and Stationery Department listed atlases, encyclopedias, dictionaries, bestselling novels, histories, children's books—and in 1897 several volumes on spirits certain to horrify temperance zealots, even as they intrigued the era's DIY mixologists:

Fleischmann's Art of Blending and Compounding Liquors and Wines. Showing how all the leading and favorite brands of whiskies, brandies, and other liquors and wines are prepared for the trade by rectifiers, etc., at the present time: with complete and correct recipes for making all the ingredients, flavorings, etc., employed in their manufacture, and the actual cost of each product as offered for sale. By Joseph Fleischmann. Publisher's price: $2.50. Our price: $1.50.

The Bordeaux Wine and Liquor Dealers' Guide. A Treatise on the Manufacture, Rectifying and Reduction of Liquors without the use of poisonous or deleterious ingredients, and on the preparation of Wines, Cordials, etc., for dealers' instruction. It includes also directions for Brewing Ales, Porter, etc., and for compounding Wines, Bitters and Punches, and Colorings and Beading for Liquors. Publisher's price: $5.00. Our price: $2.00.

2

A Chef and a Socialite Suggest . . .

While America basked in the Gilded Age, France in the later 1800s enjoyed its own Belle Epoque. Thirsts on both sides of the Pond were slaked with the advice and counsel of arbiters of taste in the kitchen and the salon.

The French "king of chefs and chef of kings," George Auguste Escoffier—known simply as Escoffier (b. 1846)—dominated continental cuisine from Paris to London from the kitchens of hotelier César Ritz. And Escoffier's influence extended across the Atlantic to Gilded Age kitchens along Fifth Avenue and, in the summer season, the "cottages" on Bellevue Avenue and Ocean Drive in Newport, Rhode Island.

Escoffier's *Guide Culinaire* (1903) swelled with upwards of three thousand recipes for every conceivable comestible from sauces to sweets. A few delectable compounds in his "Drinks and Refreshments" were free of alcohol for teetotalers and for those possibly nursing hangovers. His iced coffee (*Café Glacé*) and lemonade (*Citronade*) honor the quintessential bean and tartest citrus, and his raspberry-flavored red currant water (*Eau de Groseilles Framboisées*) is a marvel of maceration. Other beverages, however, were meant to please the palate with liqueurs, wines, or whiskey. (The quantities suggested in the recipes reproduced below were thought sufficient for fifteen servings.)

Vive la différence!

BAVARIAN CREAM—*Bavaroise*

Work eight oz. of powdered sugar with eight egg yolks in a saucepan, until the whole becomes white and reaches the *ribbon* stage. Then add consecutively: one-fifth pint of *capillary* syrup, one pint of freshly made, boiling hot tea, and the same amount of boiling milk; whipping briskly the while, that the drink may be very frothy. Complete at the last moment with one-third pint of the liqueur which is to characterize the Bavaroise; either Kirsch or Rum.

If the Bavaroise is flavored with vanilla, orange or lemon, let the flavor steep in the milk for fifteen minutes beforehand. If it be flavored with chocolate, dissolve six oz. of the latter, and add the milk to it, flavored with vanilla.

If it be coffee-flavored, set three oz. of freshly roasted and ground coffee to steep in the milk or flavor with one pint of freshly-made coffee.

Bavaroise is served in special glasses, and it must be frothy.

BISHOF—*Bischoff*

Put into a basin one bottleful of Champagne, one Sherry-glassful of "tilleul" (linden or lime) infusion, one orange and one lemon, cut into thin slices, and enough syrup at 32° to bring the preparation to 18°. Let the steeping proceed in a cool place for an hour. This done, strain; freeze it like a *Granité*, and finish it with four liqueur-glassfuls of liqueur-brandy. Serve in bumpers.

PINEAPPLE WATER—*Eau d'Ananas*

Finely chop one and a half lbs. of fresh or preserved pineapple; put it into a bowl and pour over it one quart of boiling syrup at 20°. Let it cool, and steep for two hours.

Strain through a bag; add a piece of ice and sufficient
seltzer water to reduce the liquid to 9°. Keep the preparation in a cool place for a further twenty minutes, and
complete it, when about to serve, with three liqueur-glasses
of Kirsch.

CHERRY WATER—*Eau de Cerises*

Pit two lbs. of very ripe cherries, and rub them through a sieve. Put the *purée* into a bowl with the stones, crushed in the mortar, and let the whole steep for one hours. Then moisten with one pint of filtered water, and strain the juice through a bag, or muslin folded in two and stretched.

Add a piece of well-washed ice and six oz. of sugar, and put the whole in a cool place for twenty minutes. Flavor, when about to serve, with four liqueur-glasses of Kirsch.

The saccharometer should register 9° when inserted into this preparation.

KALTSCHALE—*Kaltschale*

Peel and slice one-half lb. of peaches and an equal quantity of pineapple; add four oz. of ripe, melon pulp, cut into dice, and four oz. of a mixture of raspberries and red and white currants, cleared of their stalks. Put these fruits in a *silver timbale* and keep the latter on ice. Set a little cinnamon to steep in a half-bottleful of boiling, white wine; add half a pint of mixed *purée* of strawberries and red-currants to this infusion.

Filter the whole, and complete it by the addition of a bottle of champagne.

Pour this preparation over the fruit, and serve the *timbale* very cold.

PUNCH WITH KIRSCH—*Punch au Kirsch*

Throw a good half oz. of tea into one quart of boiling water, and let it steep for ten minutes. Put into a punch or salad-bowl one Ib. of sugar; strain the infusion of tea over the sugar, and dissolve the sugar; stirring the while with a silver spoon.

Add one and a half pints of kirsch, light it and serve in glasses.

PUNCH WITH RUM—*Punch au Rhum*

Make an infusion as above, with the same amount of tea and one quart of boiling water. Strain it over one lb. of sugar, in a punchbowl and let the sugar dissolve.

Add a few thin slices of lemon and one and a half pints of rum, and light it. Serve with a slice of lemon in each glass.

MARQUISE PUNCH—*Punch Marquise*

Put into a small, copper saucepan one quart of Sauterne wine, half-lb. of sugar, and the *zest* of the rind of one lemon bound round a clove. Dissolve the sugar; heat the wine until it becomes covered by thin white froth; and pour it into a punchbowl after having removed the *zest* and the clove.

Add half a pint of burnt brandy; light it and let it burn itself out. Serve with a thin slice of lemon in each glass.

ICE PUNCH—*Punch Glacé*

Prepare a Marquise Punch as above; when the wine is hot, take it off the fire; throw in a good half oz. of tea, and let the whole steep covered for ten minutes.

Pass the whole through a fine strainer; add one orange and one lemon; peeled and cut into slices, and some heated rum. Light it; leave to cool and reduce to 15°. Then freeze like a *Granité*, and serve in glasses.

HOT WINE—*Vins Chauds*

Pour one bottle of red wine over 10 oz. of sugar, set in a small, copper basin. Dissolve the sugar. Add one orange *zest*, a bit of cinnamon and mace, and one clove. Heat the wine until it is covered by thin froth, and then pass it through a fine strainer. Serve with a thin slice of lemon in each glass.

HOT WINE WITH ORANGE—*Vin Chaud á l'Orange*

Pour half a pint of boiling water over ten oz. of sugar. Add the *zest* of one orange and let steeping proceed for fifteen minutes. Remove the *zest*, and mix one bottle of heated Burgundy wine with the infusion.

Serve with a round slice of orange in each glass.

WINE A LA FRANCAISE—*Vin á la Française*

Put eight oz. of sugar into a salad-bowl, and sprinkle on a few tablespoons of water; that it may dissolve. Add one bottle of excellent Bordeaux wine or red Burgundy, and the half of a lemon cut into thin slices. Stir well with a silver spoon and serve with a slice of lemon in each glass.

N.B.—Always remember to free the lemons and oranges used of all seeds, which would lend a bitterness to the drink.

CLARET CUP—*Le Cup de Vin Rouge*

Put into a crystal bowl one oz. of sugar, the rind of one lemon and three slices of the latter, an equal quantity of orange, one strip of cucumber peel, one tablespoon of Angostura Bitters, and a liqueur-glass of each of the following liqueurs:—Brandy, Maraschino and white Curaçao.

Complete with one and a half bottles of red wine and a bottle of Soda. Cover and let the whole infuse. Strain, add a few pieces of very clean ice and a few leaves of fresh mint.

↤↦

On American shores, the socialite and authoress Mary Elizabeth Wilson Sherwood (Mrs. John Sherwood, b. 1826) sought to put her own stamp on the nation's cocktails. Though her contemporary female writers Louisa May Alcott and Harriet Beecher Stowe had found welcoming audiences, Wilson signed her books with the initials M. E. W., perhaps seeking the dignity and authority she suspected would be denied to a lady authoress of her time. Mrs. Sherwood had joined their ranks with such novels as *The Sarcasm of Destiny* and *Roxobel*. She also published short stories and translated poetry from the French. Now, an etiquette manual of her own, *The

Art of Entertaining (1892), arrived replete with French phrasing amid advice to American ladies who, she feared, must be the "servant-trainer, then housekeeper, wife, mother, and conversationalist," hobbled by the accident of birth that put them on the New World side of the Atlantic.

The American lady of the house, Mrs. Sherwood added, "must keep up with the always advancing spirit of the times," and in her manual she advised on all manner of beverages and their service. "The coffee-cups must be thin as egg-shells, of the most delicate French or American china. We make most delicate china and porcelain cups ourselves nowadays, at Newark, Trenton, and a dozen other places." "The cordials at the end of dinner," she likewise dictated, "must be served in cups of Russian gold filagree supporting glass. There is an analogy between the rival, luscious richness of the cordial and the cup."

"There is a vast deal of waste in offering so much wine at a ladies' lunch," she declared. "American women cannot drink much wine; the climate forbids it. We have not been brought up on beer, or on anything more stimulating than ice-water. Foreign physicians say that this is the cause of all our woes, our dyspepsia, our nervous exhaustion, our rheumatism and hysteria. I believe that climate and constitution decide these things for us. We are not prone to over-eat ourselves, to drink too much wine; and if the absence of these grosser tastes is visible in pale cheeks and thick arms, is not that better than the other extreme?"

"All entertaining can go on perfectly well without wine," she concluded, "if people so decide," and her *Art of Entertaining* advanced the "spirit" of the times with helpful recipes for beverages to provide guests with midday refreshers during the main meal of the day.

Champagne Cup: One pint bottle of soda water, one quart dry
champagne, one wine-glass of brandy, a few fresh strawberries, a peach quartered, sugar to taste; cracked ice.

Another recipe: One quart dry champagne, one pint bottle of
Rhine wine, fruit and ice as above; cracked ice. Mix in
large pitcher.

Claret Cup: One bottle of claret, one pint bottle of soda water, one wine-glass brandy, half a wine-glass of lemon-
juice, half a pound of lump sugar, a few slices of fresh
cucumber, mix in cracked ice.

Mint Julep: Fresh mint, a few drops of orange bitters and
Maraschino, a small glass of liqueur, brandy or whiskey,
put in a tumbler half full of broken ice; shake well, and
serve with fruit on top of straws.

Another recipe for Mint Julep: Half a glass of port wine, a few
drops of Maraschino, a mint, sugar, a thin slice of
lemon, shake the cracked ice from glass to glass, add
strawberry or pineapple.

Turkish Sherbets: Extract by pressure or infusion the rich
juice and fine perfume of any of the odoriferous flowers or fruits; mix them in any number or quantity to
taste. When these essences, extracts, or infusions are
prepared they may be immediately used by adding a
proper proportion of sugar or syrup; and water. Some
acid fruits, such as lemon or pomegranate, are used to
raise the flavor, but not to overpower the chief perfume. Fill the cup with cracked ice and add what wine
or spirit is preferred.

Claret Cobbler: One bottle wine, one bottle Apollinaris or
Seltzer, one lemon, half a pound of sugar; serve with ice.

Champagne Cobbler: One bottle of champagne, one half bottle of white wine, much cracked ice, strawberries, peaches or sliced oranges.

Sherry Cobbler. Full wine-glass of sherry, very little brandy, sugar, slices lemon, cracked ice. This is but one tumblerful.

Kümmel: This liqueur is very good served with shaved ice in small green claret-cups.

Punch: One bottle Arrach, one bottle brandy, two quart bottles dry champagne, one tumblerful of orange curaçao, one pound of cracked sugar, half a dozen lemons sliced, half a dozen oranges sliced. Fill the bowl with large lump of ice and add one quart of water.

Shandygaff: London porter and ginger all [ale?], half and half.

❦ 3 ❧

To-Go Cup

CROSSING THE "POND"

On the "gusty, iron-grey Sunday afternoon" of November 23, 1879, the British journalist George Sala (b. 1828), author of colorful features on travel and society for the London *Daily Telegraph*, boarded the Cunard RMS *Scythia*, bound from Liverpool to New York. Sala cut a fine figure with his trimmed Edwardian moustache and hair brushed tightly against his head, a greatcoat with plush sealskin lapels buttoned up for warmth. Eager to observe an American Thanksgiving, Sala meant to take stock of the Empire City before boarding a southbound Pullman to report on the folkways of "Dixie's Land."

Sala's coast-to-coast tour (twenty thousand miles altogether, including Chicago, Omaha, and San Francisco) would eventually put him in pursuit of the new American royalty, the "railway kings," "silver kings," "corn kings," "pork-packing kings," and "hotel kings" of America's Gilded Age. Once ashore in Gotham and registered at the Brevoort Hotel on Fifth Avenue and Eighth Street in lower Manhattan, Sala was to rhapsodize about the uniquely American November holiday, celebrated with roasted turkeys and the "traditionally orthodox dish" of "stewed cranberries." Thanksgiving, he decided, was "more than a national custom . . . it amounts to a passion."

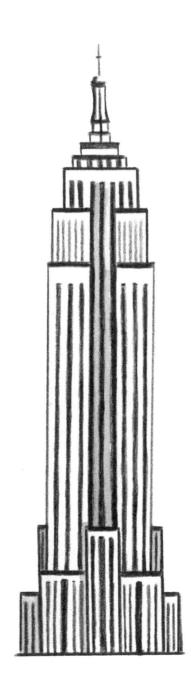

First, however, loomed the crossing on the *Scythia*, named for an ancient nomadic Central Eurasian people, and on his own voyage Sala vowed to "take the rough with the smooth." Despite "the pitching and the tossing" of the vessel, the popular journalist found himself enjoying a "comfortable state room" and a "seat at the captain's table." The Cunard liner offered the fullest of menus. For breakfast alone he might request figs, followed by broiled finnan haddie or beefsteak, poached eggs on anchovy toast, head cheese and "rolled ox tongue," or oatmeal porridge and boiled hominy with milk. The *Scythia*, Sala noted, also stocked "her wines, her spirits, her beer, and her aerated waters." Irish whiskies were featured, as were scotch, "American Rye," and "Canadian Club." Should a passenger experience seasickness—*mal de mer*—some on board suggested chicken broth. Others, however, "boldly proclaimed their belief in brandy and soda." Fortunately, the Cunard vessel offered "Brandy, Very Old."

Sala himself reported no need for the medicinal brandy and soda, neither on the *Scythia*, nor aboard the Cunard SS *Hecla* on his return voyage to Britain. But the recipe for the remedy remains a standard whether on a Cunard line or a location on terra firma.

BRANDY AND SODA

Ingredients

2 or 3 ounces brandy

Club soda or siphon

3 ice cubes

Directions

1. Pour brandy into tall glass containing ice.

2. Top with soda or siphon.

3. Stir moderately and serve.

The White Star Line—rival to Cunard—carried another literary figure in 1902, when twenty-six-year-old Jack London boarded the RMS *Majestic*, bound for England where he would write *The People of the Abyss*, a muckraking exposé of the woefully impoverished citizens of London's East End. (Just a few months later, London would become famous as the author of *The Call of the Wild*, a bestselling saga of a heroic canine's trials in the subzero Yukon winter and an American classic.) During the crossing, the Socialist writer "chummed" with his shipmates, who rallied Jack for rounds of their favorite beverage. "I was strong with youth, and unafraid," he later recalled in his autobiographical novel, *John Barleycorn* (1913). "The only thing they drank was 'horse's neck' . . . a long, soft, cool drink with an apple peel or an orange peel floating in it. And for that whole voyage," he wrote, "I drank horse's necks with my two companions."

HORSE'S NECK COCKTAIL

Ingredients

    2 ounces brandy (bourbon if preferred)

    Ginger ale

    Lemon peel (spiral peeling)

    Ice

Directions

    1. Fill tall glass with ice.

    2. Add brandy (or bourbon).

    3. Fill to top with ginger ale.

    4. Garnish with lemon spiral peel.

Not all oceanic passengers relished the onboard cocktails. The French journalist Paul Bourget struck an acerbic note when crossing the Atlantic in 1893: "There is a bar at the end of the smoking room, where the alchemist to whom is entrusted the cocktails manipulates one of those corrosive mixtures with which Americans delight to burn themselves up." (Bourget attributed the American gentlemen's graying hair and sallow complexions to "poison by the abuse of the formidable alcoholic drinks.") No doubt, the Frenchman may be forgiven for his loyalty to the vineyards of his native country.

ON THE RAILS

As the Gilded Age dawned, the railroad had turned the US and its territories into one vast rolling museum of wonders. The Great Salt Lake was not to be missed, and a two-day stopover in Chicago, the "city of the beasts," became a *must* for a gander at the marvelous stockyards. "Delightful as well as instructive," declared the railroad enthusiast Charles Nordoff, who journeyed from New York to San Francisco in 1874 and urged Americans to heed the conductor's "All aboard!"

By 1880, the American rail spanned over ninety thousand miles of track, as trains crossed plains and rivers, tunneled through mountains, eased through cities, and stopped for passenger service at major depots and Podunk towns, while the new railroad lines became American icons: the New York Central, the Erie, the Southern Pacific, the Pennsylvania ("Pennsy"), the Santa Fe, the Great Northern, and numerous others. American engineer George Pullman (b. 1831) set a new standard in train travel with his ornately decorated "hotel cars." The lavishly upholstered parlor car, sleeper cars, and club car were planned down to the last detail for passenger comfort, including fine dining and libations, and evolved in fashion from Moorish interiors to the "rustic mission style" of the turn of the century. By the early 1890s, passenger trains boasted "bath-rooms, a barber's shop . . . a library and a writing-room," and "any amount of ice for subtle internal caressing drinks made up at the bar." The railroads' profits rose, as did passengers' spirits, no matter the length of the voyage.

Sightseers boarded trains for the same conveniences that attracted cruise ship passengers in the next century and beyond. As always, transit served business travelers and others who beelined to a destination, but vacationers sought the convenience of a hotel, together with the novelty of exotic new scenery. The journey itself provided the experience, and ease and comfort were *de rigueur*. Railroad porters doubled as hotel bellmen and maids, and dining cars became dining rooms with deluxe meals and beverages, all while panoramic scenery unfolded outside the car's crystal-clear plate glass panes. From New York's capital, Albany, the New York Central cars rolled past "villages, farmhouses, and well-tilled lands," while desert cactus blooms could be spied from the windows of the Santa Fe Railroad cars in the Southwest. (The writer Henry James [b. 1843] mused that the country appeared to be made for the cars, not vice versa.)

Sightseers also sought train travel to experience the latest in modern industrial technology. A gear-and-girder boom had transformed the American landscape from fields and farms to factory zones producing eye-popping goods from sewing machines to hunting rifles and home cameras. New steel-framed buildings rose to unimaginable heights in cities across the country, and bridges spanned rivers only recently crossed by ferry. By 1900, passengers who marveled at the thundering Niagara Falls could now board the Grand Trunk

Railway to cross high above the river on "a wonder of civil engineering," the line's new high-tech single-arch, double-trestle bridge. The Grand Trunk's wine list was also wondrous, featuring a full line from the brewery, the vineyard, and the distillery.

Elsewhere, in the Pacific Northwest, travelers coursed through steep rocky canyons, fringed with evergreens and redwoods. When nearing Helena, Montana, for instance, the Great Northern skirted the creek along the jaw-dropping Prickly Pear Canyon, while passengers enjoyed beefsteaks, freshly shucked oysters, chops, and a panoply of other dishes. The wine list dazzled, with beverages ranging from Dog's Head Bass Ale to amontillado sherry, with numerous champagnes and lemonades in between. The railroad also offered fresh fish in season, and fruitcake that was produced in fifteen-ton batches to satisfy dining-car demands. The Northern Pacific came to be dubbed the "great baked potato route" because a twenty-ounce spud was the minimum weight served.

THE TUXEDO

For New Yorkers en route for a weekend in the country at Tuxedo Park, the Tuxedo cocktail was offered gratis by the Erie Railroad.

Ingredients

⅔ ounce Plymouth gin (chilled)

⅓ ounce sherry

1 dash orange bitters

Directions

1. Add gin and sherry to cocktail glass.
2. Stir.
3. Add bitters and serve.

MARTINI ACROSS THE NIAGARA RIVER

Among the cocktails to be imbibed on a journey across the Niagara River, the Grand Trunk offered the Martini, the Manhattan, and the Whiskey, each at the apparently standard railroad price of twenty cents per cocktail.

Ingredients

    2 ounces gin (chilled)

    ½ ounce Italian vermouth

    ½ ounce French vermouth

Directions

    1. Combine gin and both vermouths in martini glass.

    2. Stir.

    3. Serve with green olive.

WHISKEY SLING AT PRICKLY PEAR CANYON

Among the Great Northern's cocktails, one might select the Martini, the Manhattan, the Gin, the Whiskey Cocktail (twenty cents each), or the classic Whiskey Sling, sweetened with a simple ("gum") syrup.

Ingredients

    1 ounce whiskey (bourbon, rye, or scotch)

    2 dashes gum syrup

    Crushed ice

Directions

1. In goblet with ice, add whiskey.
2. Add gum syrup.
3. Stir, strain, and serve.

⪪ 4 ⪫

Location, Location, Location

CLUB LIFE, CLUB COCKTAILS

The gentleman's club, opined the writer and poet Francis Gerry Fairfield (b. 1836) in *The Clubs of New York* (1873), lets a man "see his friends, write his letters, and dine," preferably in the company of those politically aligned and unassailably wealthy, like himself. One devotee pronounced a man's club to be his "home," a signal of fellowship to kindred spirits and a claim certain to raise the hackles of wives and young men's mothers (and the mothers of daughters who were eager to wed and launch their own homes).

Among the most prominent clubs dotting the Gilded Age landscape (some surviving to the present) were the Bohemian Club in San Francisco, the California Club in downtown Los Angeles, the Washoe Club in Virginia City, Nevada, the Chicago Club, and numerous others, not to mention a dozen or more clubs in Manhattan, with names both suggestive and tantalizing. Shared interests were clear in the yacht and athletic clubs, while the Lotus attracted journalists, and the Blossom exalted luxurious leisure. The Union Club differed from the Union League and the Manhattan Club, and insiders monitored the jockeying of the newest Napoleons of wealth and the old guard aristocracy. New York's Knickerbocker Club, founded in 1871 and named in honor of the American author Washington Irving, numbered among the most exclusive and prestigious of private gentlemen's clubs in the Gilded Age, though in 1904 the Hotel Knickerbocker claimed the name in homage to the Dutch ancestry of the city.

With their select memberships, the men's clubs offered comfortable furniture, dining rooms, card rooms, billiard rooms, bathing facilities, and gyms for squash and handball. The "morning-room" featured the "leading" newspapers, all "temptingly laid out for perusal," together with a "well-ventilated smoking-room," optimal for "after-dinner stories and cigars of the finest brands." A gentlemen's conversation at his club ought to be "simple and conventional," wrote Francis Crowninshield (b. 1872), journalist and critic, as well as a bachelor and man-about-town, who suggested the convivial clubman propose a rubber of bridge or a cigar, but, best of all, the solicitation, "Have a drink?" "Waiter, take the orders."

Guests memorialized the libations on offer. Visiting New York City, the British journalist George Sala profiled the "palatial clubs"—the "Union, the Union League, the New York, the Manhattan, and the Athenaeum" among them— and recalled that on a certain Saturday night at the Century Club, he "met literature, art, and science in combination with stewed oysters and hot 'whiskey skins.'" When hosted at San Francisco's Bohemian Club, where drinks were served to men seated in the "most wonderful leather chairs," Jack London recalled, "Never had I heard such an ordering of liqueurs and highballs of particular brands of scotch." A Bohemian Club cocktail featuring Dubonnet, a French aperitif, was on the menu in November 1914, but the Highball was a staple of the bar.

"The perfect clubman is another word for the perfect gentleman," insisted socialite and author Emily Post (b. 1872) in her essential guide, *Etiquette in Society, in Business, in Politics, and at Home*, first published in 1922. He never allows himself to show "irritability to anyone" and "makes it a point to be courteous to a new member or a guest." What's more, he "scrupulously observes the rules of the club," including the prompt payment of all dues and debts, "always with an instinctive horror of sponging." As women's clubs sprang up in the early 1900s, it is not inconceivable that some ladies envisioned their own signature beverages. For the time being, the all-purpose Club Cocktail, listed in *The Old Waldorf-Astoria Bar Book*, would do.

THE KNICKERBOCKER

Ingredients

> 1 wineglass Jamaica rum
> 1 dash curaçao
> 3 dashes raspberry syrup
> Juice of ½ lemon or lime
> Cracked ice

Directions

> 1. Squeeze lemon or lime into mixing glass with small amount of ice.
> 2. Add all other ingredients.
> 3. Stir well, stain, and serve in fancy glass.

JAMAICA HIGHBALL AT THE BOHEMIAN CLUB

Ingredients

½ cocktail glass Jamaica rum

2 lumps ice

Slice lemon or lime

Directions

1. Add ice to tall glass.
2. Add rum.
3. Fill with siphon and garnish with lemon or lime.

WHISKY SKIN COCKTAIL AT THE CENTURY CLUB

Ingredients

> 2 ounces scotch whisky
>
> 4 ounces water at boiling point
>
> I teaspoon sugar
>
> Lemon peel

Directions

> 1. Pour water and sugar into tumbler.
> 2. Add whisky.
> 3. Squeeze peel to release citrus oil, add, and serve.

CLUB COCKTAIL

Ingredients

> ⅔ ounce Tom gin
>
> ⅓ ounce vino vermouth
>
> I dash green Chartreuse
>
> 2 dashes gum syrup
>
> 2 dashes orange bitters
>
> Ice

Directions

> 1. Fill tall glass halfway with ice.
> 2. Add all ingredients.
> 3. Stir well, strain, and serve in cocktail glass.

THE COUNTRY HOUSE

Wedged between "winter" and "summer" on the social calendar, the "between-season" was prime time for house parties in the countryside. The months from November through earliest spring were spent in the city, where Society (those of the highest social rank) enjoyed parties, balls, and evenings at the theater. The summer season meant six weeks—early

July through August—in coastal Newport, Rhode Island, or Bar Harbor, Maine, where yachting, golf, and racquet sports punctuated nighttime parties and galas. The "between-season" weeks, however, became optimal for country house parties. The guests, invited customarily for three or four days, arrived by carriage, rail, or, in the early 1900s, by motorcar. Some were close friends or family members of the host and hostess, others barely acquainted, and still others, especially among the younger set, total strangers.

No matter. According to Emily Post's *Etiquette*, the house accommodated "only" those "whose owners belong equally to best society," and Mrs. Post presumed that the guests, like "all people of good position," would "talk alike, behave alike and live alike." Under the benign watch of the host and hostess, guests were welcomed, freed to enjoy themselves, and expected to appear punctually, in formal attire, at dinner.

Cocktails oiled the social wheels. "The hostess at a large country house," said Francis Crowninshield, a frequent, sought-after guest, "is naturally expected to provide all the weekend essentials," including "liquors." Young bachelors were known to imbibe, he observed, from the beginning of the day. A single young man, waking in the guest room in the morning, would "demand" that a servant bring him a "bracer," preferably "a brandy and soda," to preface his "breakfast and a cigar." A gentleman of any age, unaccompanied by his valet but awake in the earliest "barnyard hours," was advised by Emily Post to carry "a small solidified alcohol outfit" to start the day "without disturbing anyone." Breakfast at a Gilded Age house party might include eggs, oatmeal, shredded wheat, rolls, muffins, toast, fruit, coffee, tea, chocolate, milk—and Milk Punch, if not the formidable, but popular,

Brain-Duster or Black Velvet. "As regards midday beverages," recalled a British visitor, "one's brain reels at fond memories of . . . Remsen refreshers."

The arbiter of etiquette, Emily Post, liberally dispensed house party dos and don'ts in her bible of behavior. Growing up in Tuxedo Park, a planned community of country cottages designed by her architect father, Bruce Price, on land that had been purchased in 1885 by tobacco baron Pierre Lorillard IV as a private hunting-and-fishing preserve for wealthy New Yorkers just beyond the city limits, she took copious mental notes on Tuxedo's hosts and their guests. (Whether the Native American word *tucsedo*, meaning "crooked river," was known to Emily and her set, her promotion of the comfortable men's dinner suit favored at Tuxedo Park has given the suit an enduring linguistic primacy over the park.)

On sunny days, country house guests amused themselves on the tennis and croquet courts, on the archery field, and in the saddle on horses provided by the host. Perhaps they strolled the gardens or spent a few hours seated comfortably on the veranda. Unfavorable weather meant the bridge table indoors, nestling with the latest popular books, and chatting in lightest conversation. ("Think before you speak. . . . Do not be always witty. . . . Never make yourself the hero or heroine of your own story.")

Despite the tribute to society's "best," Emily Post's *Etiquette* imposed a near-martial law on the country house party. Before inviting anyone, the hostess ought to spend at least one night in each guest room to test its comfort. Every guest deserved a full bathroom with "hot water faucets that are not seemingly jokes of the plumber." Beyond towels, the highly recommended toiletries included violet water, bath salts, Listerine, talcum powder, and a razor strop. Upon arrival, the guests were to be shown to their rooms to freshen up, and to be "supplied with tea, sandwiches, cakes, and whatever the tea-table affords." One hostess immediately served champagne, complaining that guests are "dull as dishwater. . . . till the champagne comes."

The tell-all memoir *Confessions of a Social Secretary* (1917), by Corinne Low, offers a bird's-eye view of such house parties held at Glenclyffe Farms by the compulsively sociable Mamie Fish (b. 1853), one of the most notable hostesses of the Gilded Age. The wife of Stuyvesant Fish, president of the Illinois Central Railroad and son of a former governor of New York, also entertained at the couple's grand home on the corner of Madison Avenue and Seventy-Eighth Street in New York City, designed by the architect Stanford White, as well as at Crossways, their so-called "cottage" in Newport, the summer capital of elite Society. But if the winter and summer seasons were spoken for, the "in-between" weeks were optimal for house parties at their "fine old place on the Hudson, across from West Point."

Guests arrived along "a private road lined with . . . beeches and oaks" to reach "a long, low house, surrounded by spotless verandas" and a view of the Hudson River "as it curved like a supple blade." Delectable dinners and dancing were promised, and often an evening entertainment by a musical troupe or magician. Over four days, the cocktail count multiplied furiously. The young Society bachelor, dreading boredom, typically arrived at Glenclyffe feeling "parched" and immediately summoned his host's butler in a "tone of authority" to request, "Cocktail, please." His "amber-colored drink" arrived in moments, "fairly rocking with the solicitous haste of its delivery." The "amber" hue hints of a "brown" liquor, a bourbon or rye, and the "haste" implies an easy, fast mix. Mamie, though, often brooded about expenses, from the outlandish butcher's bill to the exorbitant costs of uniformed footmen's liveries. Her secretary recalled the careful household budgeting, down to the "SERVANTS'" wages, for "THE BUTLER'S DRESS SUIT," and "A DOLLAR FOR A COCKTAIL."

"It is thrilling," said Frank Crowninshield, "to receive the invitation" to a house party" and to set forth "full of expectant pleasure." But the "most welcome part of it all," he concluded, "is the moment of departure." His hostess might agree with the Arabian law of hospitality: "Welcome the coming, speed the parting guest." When one guest complained, noting an insufficient stock of bath towels, that "I had to dry myself on the bath-mat," Mamie Fish rejoined, "Indeed! You were lucky not to be afforded the door-mat!" Both hosts and guests, nevertheless, continued to play their parts in the annual social drama of the "between-season," assuaged no doubt by a steady supply of cocktails.

MILK PUNCH

Ingredients

> 8 ounces milk
>
> ⅔ ounce Santa Cruz rum
>
> ⅓ ounce brandy
>
> 1 dash vanilla extract
>
> 1 teaspoon sugar
>
> Ice chips
>
> Nutmeg (if desired)

Directions

> 1. In large glass or shaker, add milk.
> 2. Add all other ingredients.
> 3. Shake well, strain, and serve.

THE BRAIN-DUSTER

Ingredients

> 1 ounce absinthe
>
> 2 dashes Italian vermouth
>
> 2 dashes sherry
>
> 2 dashes gum syrup
>
> 1 lime
>
> Ice

Directions

> 1. In mixing tumbler, squeeze juice of lime.
> 2. Add all other ingredients.
> 3. Stir, strain, and serve.

BLACK VELVET

Ingredients

> 2 ounces champagne
>
> 2 ounces porter

Directions

> 1. In champagne flute, add champagne.
> 2. Top with porter and serve.

REMSEN

Ingredients

> 1 jigger Tom gin
>
> Soda water
>
> Lemon peel (whole lemon)
>
> Ice

Directions

> 1. Add gin to ice-filled tall glass.
> 2. Add lemon.
> 3. Fill with soda, stir, and serve.

WHISKEY FRAPPÉ

Ingredients

> 1 ounce whiskey (bourbon or rye)
>
> 2 dashes gum syrup
>
> Ice

Directions

> 1. Fill glass with ice as desired.
> 2. Add whiskey and gum syrup.
> 3. Still or shake vigorously and serve.

SUNDAY TEA AT 840 FIFTH AVENUE

The most sought-after address on a Gilded Age invitation, hands down, was the French Renaissance château overlooking Central Park at the corner of East Sixty-Fifth Street in New York City. Within its ornate, mirrored walls, the guests at 840 Fifth Avenue were seated upon antique furniture arranged on marble flooring spread with tiger skin rugs and rare Persian carpets. Gold-framed, classical paintings covered the walls, crystal chandeliers sparkled, and numerous vases of American Beauty roses reminded guests that their hostess was sometimes called the Mystic Rose. In this space, Caroline Astor—known always as Mrs. Astor—ruled over Society with a "scepter she held firmly, absolutely, and charmingly," as one socialite observed. Her demeanor of "imperial grandeur" reminded one admirer of Marie de Medici.

Wealthy from birth, Caroline Schermerhorn (b. 1830) had married the even wealthier William Backhouse Astor, Jr. (the grandson of John Jacob Astor), and soon presided over the social crème de la crème of Gilded Age America known as the Four Hundred (a number said to be comfortable keeping company with one another in Mrs. Astor's ballroom).

Ever gracious, Mrs. Astor was in residence on Fifth Avenue from late autumn to earliest spring, after which she traveled to England and the Continent, visited friends, was fitted for gowns at the Parisian couturier Worth, and prepared for the summer season in Newport, before readying for the next New York winter season of opera, theater, parties, and balls. Mrs. Astor's ball was the most exclusive, premier event of the year, held annually on the last Monday night in January.

On Sunday afternoons in New York, Mrs. Astor received guests for tea in her "small, downstairs Louis XV salon." Francis Crowninshield, the founding editor of *Vanity Fair* magazine and a devoted admirer, often attended. Mrs. Astor poured the tea by her own hand, as Crowninshield recalled, and "allowed her butler to pour livelier libations for the varied retinue of men of all ages, who came . . . to pay her their devoirs." The unnamed "libations" are a matter of speculation. Mrs. Astor's butler would see to the required volume, but a single serving is as follows:

HOT BENEFACTOR

Ingredients

    4 ounces boiling-hot water

    2–3 lumps sugar

    ½ ounce Jamaica rum

    3 ounces Chianti

    1 slice lemon

    Nutmeg

Directions

    1. In hot-punch glass or cup, add sugar and water.

    2. Add rum, Chianti, and lemon.

    3. Grate nutmeg on top and serve.

SARATOGA SPRINGS

"The worthy, the fashionable, the daring . . . flock to the Springs," declared Washington Irving (b. 1783), the writer whose "Legend of Sleepy Hollow" had terrified countless children with its tale of a headless horseman haunting the environs of New York City. Like others in the early 1800s, Irving disapproved of such leisure travel, fearing it would ruin the young nation's morals. He apparently did not know that Mohawk tribesmen and women had ventured for centuries into the "medicine springs of the Great Spirit" nestled in the Adirondacks to seek relief from aches and pains by bathing in the healing thermal waters.

By the Gilded Age, few recalled that *Adirondack* was a Mohawk word, and the onetime Native American healing site had become a premier American resort, the "Queen of Spas." Housed in architected buildings, the rival commercial bot-

tlers now had pump houses, attendants, and their own com-
peting brands of effervescent spring water. Hotels and retail
establishments flourished, as did casino gambling and horse
racing. Celebrities such as Diamond Jim Brady and musical
theater star Lillian Russell mixed with industrial titans at the
track and the roulette wheel. Some guests followed their six-
week Newport summer season with a restorative few weeks
at the Springs, lamenting that "too many parties, too little
exercise and too much rich food had their inevitable effect on
tempers." The water cure, they hoped, would "prevent half
of New York society being at loggerheads" in the upcoming
winter social season.

Visitors from the hinterlands could travel to the Springs
by train, and New Yorkers might board the New York Central north from the city—or, if time permitted, enjoy cruis-
ing on the Citizens' Steamboat Company's *Saratoga* for much
of the two-hundred-mile trip up the Hudson River. Unlike
the crowded, dangerous steamboats that Mark Twain had described in his novel about Huckleberry Finn on the Mississippi River, the *Saratoga* provided ample amenities to ensure
pleasure for all but the most discontented traveler. "It is only
in the steamer," one traveler wrote, "that the Hudson can be
truly perceived and enjoyed. . . . The traveler who loves the
law of beauty and pursues pleasure will take the steamer and
secure silence, cleanliness, sufficient speed, and an unen-
cumbered enjoyment of the land."

Steaming up the picturesque Hudson in 1900, the *Saratoga*
offered the finest accommodations, a restaurant serving evening
supper (à la carte) from 5:00 to 9:30 p.m., and a wine list to
expand the imagination with burgundies, sauternes, and Rhine
wines, or one of the nine imported champagnes ("American

champagnes" listed separately: Urbana and Cook's). The vessel's "Sunset Wines" suggested the hour for sipping, and otherwise passengers could choose "Clarets," "Cordials," and "Malt Liquors," or beers and ales of numerous brands. (A "Mount Vernon Whiskey" and curiously titled "Antediluvian Whiskey" might equally appeal.) Four cocktails were offered onboard: the Whiskey, the Martini, the Manhattan, and the Tom Gin.

TOM GIN COCKTAIL

Ingredients

> 1 ounce Tom gin (chilled)
>
> 1 dash orange bitters

Directions

> 1. Pour gin into chilled martini glass.
> 2. Add bitters.

Once disembarked at the Springs, elite vacationers registered at the Grand Union or the United States Hotel, which boasted accommodations for one thousand guests—"without taking account of such entries as . . . 'William K. Vanderbilt, wife, two maids, two dogs, and fifteen horses.'" Socialite Elizabeth Drexel Lehr (later in life, Lady Decies) fondly recalled the "magnificence" of the "Hotel United States," where her family had summered for years. The hotel stairs "seemed to pour . . . with grandeur down to the street," where "Society sat enthroned upon the piazza." (One glimpse of a lady *en costume*: "a superb gown of brocade silk with a Worth collar, sleeve puffs and skirt panels of heliotrope violate [purple] richly embroidered.")

The demands of fashion dictated that a lady arrive with a "Saratoga trunk," necessarily carried by "two stout men." Eliza beth Lehr noted that Saratoga "was a Spa, but some of her fame rested solidly upon the trunk named for her," which she deemed "an institution" (the eponymous luggage would in 1941 provide the title for a bestselling novel by Edna Ferber). "There is extravagance at Saratoga," one memoirist sniped, "but if you take away . . . everything that is only worn for fashion's sake, we should hardly need any civilization, much less a Saratoga."

Fine dining at the major hotels was assured (the "Saratoga potato" became famous as the potato chip) and bracing beverages awaited guests and cottagers who had no need to import supplies for the cocktail hour, for the Saratoga retailer J. H. Farrington advertised "on hand a full line of Liquors, Brandies, Gins, Wines, &c." Those vacationers whose cocktails were mixed by bartender Len Stockwell enjoyed a terpsichorean bonus, for behind the bar of the United States Hotel Stockwell "could shake a Saratoga cocktail to the perfect rhythm of his own clog-dancing."

THE SARATOGA COCKTAIL

Ingredients

> 1 ounce rye or bourbon whiskey
>
> 1 ounce brandy
>
> 1 ounce vermouth
>
> 2 dashes Angostura bitters
>
> Ice
>
> ¼ lemon slice

Directions

> 1. Combine ingredients.
> 2. Shake well with 2 small lumps of ice.
> 3. Serve with lemon slice.

While at Saratoga, Elizabeth's father "took the baths at Magnetic Spring," and she named other spas: High Rock, Red Star, and "a certain Sulphur spring at which my mother would occasionally dismount from her horse to taste with a wry face." "I suppose there were a few who really came to drink the water," she pondered, but she failed to recall details of "those long hours of discussion about the different treatments and their success which you hear at most watering places." It has been reported that gentlemen bathers, luxuriating in the five-foot deep pools of effervescent spring water, enjoyed Mint Juleps served on floating cork trays.

BRANDY JULEP

Ingredients

    I ounce cognac

    I dash Jamaica rum

    Ice (crushed)

    Mint sprigs

Directions

1. Add cognac and rum to large ice-filled goblet.
2. In small mixing glass, bruise mint with a little water and sugar.
3. Crush mint, sugar, and water mix with muddler and strain into goblet.
4. Add rum.
5. Stir.
6. Dress with fresh mint springs and, if desired, with fruit.

AN OLD-FASHIONED DINNER PARTY

The American novelist Willa Cather (b. 1873) is known largely for novels like *O! Pioneers*, panoramic stories of the Midwest featuring heroic, sod-busting immigrant homesteaders who wrest a living from the fecund prairies. Bound for the bakery, Cather's "amber waves of grain" bypass the distillery. But another scenario plays out in Cather's novel *A Lost Lady*, set in a small Western railroad town during the 1890s, when Grover Cleveland occupied the White House.

On one pleasant evening, guests assemble at the fine old home of retired railroad executive Captain Forrester, his stylishly beautiful and much younger (and flirtatious) wife, a local judge and his nephew, and the Ogdens, a wealthy, stolid couple, with their rosy-complexioned daughter, Constance, who is apt to pout when displeased. The party also includes bachelor Frank Ellinger, a tall, dark rake of forty whose physique shows to advantage in his "white waistcoat" and "conspicuously well-cut dinner coat." Cather's nods to bottles of champagne, brandy, and sherry signal that alcoholic refreshments are customarily served in the Forrester home—and in the appropriate glassware.

Tension smolders between Frank and Mrs. Forrester when the bachelor emerges from the dining room "with a glittering tray full of cocktails" and offers up a Gilded Age classic to energize Cather's plot. "They were old-fashioned whiskey cocktails," the delectations prepared by the bachelor to promote "general conversation." With a "pouty smile," the underage Constance Ogden rejects a proferred "little dish of Maraschino cherries." "No, I don't want those," she says, while plucking the whiskey-flavored fruit from the bottom of Frank's glass. "I like it to taste of something."

Mrs. Forrestor has only plaudits for the mixologist. "Very good, Frank, very good," proclaims the host, asking, "Are encores in order?" Indeed they are: "one more round for everybody."

THE OLD FASHIONED

Ingredients

> 2 ounces rye or bourbon
>
> 2 dashes Angostura bitters
>
> 1 sugar cube
>
> Maraschino cherry
>
> Club soda

Directions

> 1. Place the sugar cube in an Old Fashioned glass.
> 2. Wet it down with Angostura bitters and a short splash of club soda.
> 3. Crush the sugar with a wooden muddler, then rotate the glass so that the sugar grains and bitters give it a liquid lining.
> 4. Add Maraschino cherry.
> 5. Add large ice cube or cubes.

6. Pour in the whiskey.
7. Add seltzer (soda) water.
8. Garnish with an orange twist, and serve with a stirring rod if desired.

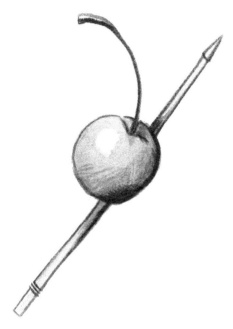

AFLOAT WITH A FRIEND

The young postmaster in Harold, California, did not dream how the fan letter he was about to pen to an unknown writer in 1899 would change his life. Sorting the US mail in the speck of a town near the western edge of the Mojave Desert, the handsome, dark-eyed young postmaster with a cleft chin and handlebar moustache—improbably named Cloudesley Johns—had recently read a short story called "To the Man on Trail" in the *Overland Monthly*, a magazine published in San

Francisco to showcase Western writers, and now he wanted to let its author know how much he had enjoyed it.

"To the Man on Trail," he wrote, vividly depicted "a barren struggle with cold and death" in the Yukon Territory during the gold rush of 1897–98. As Cloudesley opened the *Overland Monthly*, the blistering Mojave gave way to the Yukon and he "escaped" to a fictional cabin on Christmas Day, where gold miners gathered for spiked punch and storytelling. The sudden "Crack!" of a sled-dog whip announced the arrival of the title character, a six-foot-two "personage" whose brows and eyelashes were "white with ice" from hours driving in subzero weather. Cloudesley easily pictured the "wolfskin cap," the "mackinaw jacket," and the "beaded belt" that held "two large Colt revolvers and a hunting-knife," plus a sled-dog "whip" and large-bore rifle. Reading further, he recognized the well-crafted tension, sharp descriptions, and the feeling of the assembled comrades' developing allegiance to the "Man on Trail"—all winning Cloudesley Johns's admiration and prompting the very first fan letter that the story's author, Jack London, ever received.

The two became pen pals, renewed their friendship whenever possible, and remained lifelong friends. An aspiring writer himself, Cloudesley sent manuscript drafts to Jack, who offered constructive criticism. Alas, Cloudesley's budding literary career withered due to his demanding schedule as a newspaper reporter in Los Angeles, where he had relocated, and he often abandoned the writer's desk for hours to organize Socialist Party meetings in Southern California. As Socialists, both men forged shared political views from their crushing stints of manual labor. Jack had toiled in a jute mill, a cannery, and a steam laundry, while Cloudesley laid rails in the blazing Southern California desert sun for the Southern Pacific Railroad, trapped by a foreman who closely rationed the water, lest the workers flee.

By 1906, Cloudesley's friend was famous, the author of more than a dozen books of fiction, investigative journalism, war correspondence, and essays. Magazine sales rocketed with a featured story by Jack London, and royalties supported London's purchase of a California ranch in Sonoma (translation: Valley of the Moon). Remarried and the father of two daughters by his first wife, London also anchored a sloop, the *Spray*, for getaway sailing on the San Francisco Bay and the waters of the Sacramento Delta.

In 1906, Cloudesley's friend invited him to "recreate" for six weeks on the *Spray*, and Cloudesley jumped at the chance. Under sail or anchored for the night, the two friends engaged in long political discussions and read passages aloud to one another from *The Theory of the Leisure Class*, Thorstein Veblen's tart critique of the manners and mores of the rich. London had stowed whiskey by the gallon for the six-week sojourn, and Jack reported that he and his pal drank Hot Toddies regularly, "one before breakfast, one before dinner, one before supper, and a final one before we went to bed."

"We never got drunk," Jack wrote, "but I will say that four times a day we were very genial." The toddies, he added, produced "the most exhilarating kick imaginable."

THE HOT TODDY

Ingredients

> 8 ounces hot water
>
> 2 ounces whiskey (preferably bourbon)
>
> 1 tablespoon honey
>
> 1 teaspoon lemon juice
>
> 1 lemon slice

Directions

> 1. Pour hot water into mug.
> 2. Add honey, whiskey, and lemon juice.
> 3. Stir.
> 4. Garnish with lemon slice.

❧ 5 ❧

Spirited Cities

NEW YORK

"New York is one of the most wonderful products of our wonderful western civilization," rhapsodized Union officer turned prolific travel author Willard Glazer (b. 1841) in *Peculiarities of American Cities* (1883). After visiting more than twenty American cities from Pittsburgh to Savannah, Glazer found New York, "a world in itself," the "monetary, scientific, artistic and intellectual centre of the western world." Unknown to Glazier, Gotham had also become the cocktail capital of Gilded Age America.

Welcoming "almost every nationality within its boundaries" and amplifying "almost every tongue spoken," by the Gilded Age New York had outlived its Dutch colonial origins, its chapter in the American Revolution, and its notorious ("sanguinary") riots, such as the Draft Riots of 1863 triggered by the Conscription Act. The city had also weathered the flagrant political and financial corruption of the Tammany Hall regime of William Marcy ("Boss") Tweed (b. 1823). While lamenting that New York contained "much that is evil," Glazer insisted that it "abounds with more that is good," hailing it as a modern city thoroughly "cosmopolitan in its character."

The march of mansions along Fifth Avenue had only begun when Glazier took notes in the mid-1880s, but he pronounced it "the most splendid avenue in America." ("No plebeian horse cars are permitted to disturb its well-bred quiet," for "the rumble of elegant equipages is alone heard upon its . . . pavement.") Brilliant architecture had kept pace throughout the city, including "magnificent" public buildings and high-rise office towers. An admirable "granite" Congregational Church complemented the "Roman Catholic Cathedral of St. Patrick" (just completing its towers) and the "Jewish Temple Emanuel, the finest specimen of Moorish architecture in the country."

Edifying recreation awaited patrons of Booth's Theatre at the corner of Sixth Avenue and Twenty-Third Street, "the most magnificent place of amusement in America," while New Yorkers were invited to step away from the urban bustle to enjoy Central Park, the former marshy, rocky wasteland, completed in 1876, that now comprised 843 acres of trees and shrubbery, drives, walks, a zoological gardens, inspirational statues of "celebrated American and European Statesmen and poets," and the ancient Egyptian obelisk known as Cleopatra's Needle. So popular was the park, Glazer found, that visitors had to "elbow" their way among the crowds, perhaps to line up for ice cream or ale at the Dairy. Wall Street struck the visitor as a "gigantic" gambling casino, "the great monetary centre of the entire country," extending "to every section . . . of the world."

Though Glazer mapped the city's streets, squares, and neighborhoods, he described little of interest to the epicure or imbiber, though two memorable establishments were to be found in the area around Madison Square. Delmonico's restaurant, established by two Swiss brothers in the 1830s, taught both old and new money New York the difference between eating and fine dining. As Manhattan Island became Gotham, the Italian-Swiss Delmonico brothers, Giovanni and Pietro, expanded from their successful restaurant in the financial district to add the more posh establishment that Glazer observed, with its first-floor café, private dining rooms, and "regal" red-and-gold ballroom. In addition to its signature dishes—lobster Newburg, eggs Benedict, and baked Alaska ("ice cream in an envelope of whipped cream, the whole toasted in the oven!")—the Delmonico wine list was unsurpassed in the city (many bottles bearing the house label). In the era of the cocktail, however, Delmonico's bowed to contemporary taste.

Glazer's guidebook also listed the Hoffman House near Madison Square, under the proprietorship of Edward ("Ed" or "Ned") Stokes (b. 1841). The hotel had become notorious when, in 1871, the voluptuous Josie Mansfield, Stokes's current mistress, flirted with her longtime lover and patron, "Robber Baron" Jim Fisk (b. 1835), of the notorious Erie Railroad stock schemes. "Decked out in his best haberdashery," "Jubilee" Jim sought the company of the lady, whereupon the jealous Stokes raised a pistol and shot him dead. Claiming self-defense and emotional turmoil, Stokes was tried for murder, retried after a hung jury, and tried a third time when his death sentence was overturned on appeal. He served four years of a six-year sentence in Sing Sing prison, then promptly took up the hospitality business.

Under Stokes's hand, the Hoffman House's spectacular barroom was known as "the most famous loafing-place for business, professional, and sporting men in the late afternoons and evenings." The Hoffman was famed for its "great bar . . . of exceptional length, and a huge oil painting . . . of mythological nudities which seemed to appeal particularly to gentlemen in their cups." A good many such "cups" contained cocktails named for the hotel. Stokes, what's more, is credited with the invention of the city's own cocktail, the namesake beverage soon to become a classic served on oceangoing steamships and railroad passenger cars, and in private homes and at restaurants nationwide. "Ned Stokes's flamboyant and voluptuous tastes," insisted one chronicler, made the "focal point" of the men's bar the Manhattan.

THE DELMONICO

Ingredients

  ½ ounce Plymouth gin

  ½ ounce French vermouth

  1 dash orange bitters

  2 slices orange peel

  Ice

Directions

  1. In tall glass filled with ice, add gin and vermouth.

  2. Add bitters.

  3. Squeeze orange peel over the top to release citrus oil.

  4. Stir.

  5. Strain into martini glass.

  6. Garnish with second orange peel.

THE HOFFMAN HOUSE

Ingredients

  1½ ounces Plymouth gin

  ½ ounce French vermouth

  2 dashes orange bitters

  Ice

  Lemon peel

Directions

1. Combine gin, vermouth, and bitters in ice-filled shaker.
2. Shake and strain into martini glass
3. Squeeze lemon peel over top to release citrus oil.

THE MANHATTAN

Ingredients

½ ounce Irish whiskey

½ ounce Italian vermouth

2 dashes orange bitters

2 pinches refined sugar or I teaspoon simple syrup

Ice

Directions

1. Add whiskey and vermouth to ice-filled tall glass or shaker.
2. Add sugar.
3. Add bitters.
4. Stir and strain into martini glass.

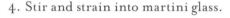

Rivals to Stokes's Hoffman House inevitably challenged its claim to supremacy in the world of Gilded Age cocktails, both shaken and stirred—and, what's more, served in an atmosphere of opulence. In 1893, the stunning high-rise Waldorf Hotel, built by the fabulously wealthy William Waldorf Astor (b. 1848), opened at the corner of Fifth Avenue and Thirty-Fourth Street. It was a "veritable palace," according to the *New York Times*. Under the innovative hotelier George C. Boldt (b. 1851), who had previously managed the Philadelphia Club and the thousand-room Bellevue-Stratford Hotel, the Waldorf's Men's Café opened its doors in "an elaborate room with panels of dark oak and much handsomely carved woodwork," as rumors circulated that "patrons were expected to learn that drinking cocktails might be done while sitting."

Instead of leaning against the time-honored "stand-up" bar, here gentleman "could sit in a luxurious armchair at a small table, with friends." A large fireplace at one end of the room cheered the space with crackling oak logs, and waiters roasted potatoes in the embers for patrons to enjoy with their drinks. With or without a hot spud, customers learned that "a gentleman did not need to rest one foot on a brass rail in order to enjoy his afternoon cocktail."

Not four years later, a second grand hotel rose next door on the southwest corner of Thirty-Fourth Street, cheek by jowl to the Waldorf. Towering over its rival by four stories, the new sixteen-story Astoria Hotel was built by William's much-loathed archrival, John Jacob Astor IV (b. 1864), the son of Society's "Queen," who was known simply as "Mrs. Astor." Designed by the same architect who had blueprinted the Waldorf, the newer hotel, like its predecessor, was fashioned in the German Renaissance style. When its doors opened in

1897, the manager of the new Astoria Hotel was none other than George Boldt, who had bolted the Waldorf to become the majordomo of the Astoria.

Bowing to patrons' demands, Boldt restored the traditional bar at the new venue so that its clientele might imbibe with one foot on the brass rail running below while bartenders mixed and served the drinks in plain sight. Eyeing potential revenue from Wall Street, the ingenious manager installed bull and bear statues, cast in bronze, at opposing ends of the mahogany bar, while a glass-domed ticker tape machine in one corner quietly tracked the latest stock valuations and sales volume.

The strategy worked. The new bar became the after-hours haunt of Wall Streeters who, after a grueling session at the stock exchange, descended on the bar where they "staked fortunes," "formed pools," and "plotted to corner markets." Shoulder-to-shoulder, drinks in hand, the "financiers and market operators" were "willing to bet on anything, and to any amount." Celebrities such as William ("Buffalo Bill") Cody added zest, and one patron recalled "an influx of rough-looking men in wide-brimmed hats" and "cowboy boots," boasting of their "'big strikes.'" They "wanted the most expensive drinks," recalled one chronicler, and "in mining camps from Mexico to Alaska" "Boldt's bar" became "known all over the world."

In 1897, the feud between the cousins became a truce when the prospect of redoubled profits from a combined hotel proved irresistible to both sons of the House of Astor. The two buildings of the Waldorf-Astoria were connected in grand style by a marble-paneled, red-carpeted, Corinthian-columned corridor dubbed Peacock Alley, where the famed and the fashionable paraded, while admirers, seated comfortably on leather banquettes, gawked from the sidelines. Monsieur Boldt, who reportedly "knew where the social power and money lay, and how to massage it," soon managed the combined hotel, the Waldorf-Astoria (soon nicknamed the Hyphen). Henry James called the hotel "a perfect riot of creation."

As the First World War loomed in January 1914, the Waldorf-Astoria menu celebrated the ingenuity of the passing Gilded Age's mixologists and the patrons who repeatedly raised a glass in tribute. Among the selections: the Vermouth Cocktail, Gin Cocktail, Manhattan, Dewey Cocktail, Martini, Whiskey Cocktail, Whiskey Punch, Rum Punch, Rum Sour, Whiskey Sour, Gin Sour, and Southern Sour, among numerous punches and cobblers. To each his or her own, but the signature cocktail was, of course, the Waldorf-Astoria.

THE WALDORF

Ingredients

> ½ ounce whiskey (bourbon or rye)
>
> ½ ounce Italian vermouth
>
> $1/6$ ounce absinthe
>
> 1 dash Manhattan bitters
>
> Ice

Directions

> 1. Combine ingredients in ice-filled tall glass.
> 2. Stir.
> 3. Strain into chilled martini glass.

THE ASTORIA

Ingredients

> 1 ounce Tom gin
>
> 2 ounces French vermouth

2 dashes orange bitters

Ice

Directions

1. In ice-filled tall glass add gin and vermouth.

2. Add bitters.

3. Stir and strain into martini glass.

THE WALDORF-ASTORIA

Ingredients

1 ounce Bénédictine (iced)

Whipped cream

Directions

1. Add Bénédictine to martini glass.

2. Cover and mound whipped cream on top.

CHICAGO

Chicago bartenders' creative urges had long been stifled by the city's reputation for hard-driving businessmen and burly workers who favored a shot and a beer "chaser" in watering holes along Whiskey Row, a blocks-long battery of saloons just outside the meatpacking plants. Frivolous cocktails were thought best relegated to luxe resorts like Saratoga.

Never discount the creativity of a bartender besotted with a fair maiden, however, whose appearance onstage might provide the right inspiration. In 1888, the vaudeville actress Mamie Taylor appeared in Chicago in a stage rendition of H. Rider Haggard's bestselling novel *She*, the tale of a lost African kingdom ruled by a feminist queen. Onstage in the role of Delyesha (a character nowhere in the novel), Miss Taylor captivated a bartender who combined scotch whisky, ginger ale, and lime juice in honor of the actress. Whether the honoree imbibed the eponymous beverage remains an open question. A kindred effervescent libation appears in the novel *The Woman That's Good* (1900), a cautionary tale of appetites both erotic and alcoholic, where we find a gentleman in a hotel on Chicago's Michigan Avenue "absorbing a very long and comforting drink. . . . the divinest morning drink invented by those suave assassins, the barkeepers," and "known to the initiated as a 'gin fizz.'"

The legacy of Chicago's true Gilded Age splendor, however, would rest on the immense popularity of a world-class attraction. In the summer of 1893, no one could compete with the Windy City. From spring into the fall, Chicago triumphed over Coney Island, Niagara Falls, and Atlantic City's beachfront boardwalk as the nation's most popular vacation hotspot. In the city's Jackson Park, along the south shore of Lake Michigan, visitors surged to the site of the World's Columbian Exposition, where 686 acres of exhibitions extolled the "progress of human civilization." The turnstiles counted nearly one-quarter of the US population—twenty-seven million visitors—at the Chicago fair, marking four centuries since Christopher Columbus had "discovered" America.

Winning the competition against other American cities (including New York), Chicago zealously determined to use the exposition to showcase its recovery from the Great Fire of 1871, which had killed more than three hundred people and destroyed a vast swath of the city, and the 1886 Haymarket Riot, when a bomb thrown during a labor strike sent shockwaves throughout the country, spreading fear that anarchists were on the march. The Columbian Exposition in Chicago would surpass all previous fairs, including the 1889 Exposition Universelle in Paris, with its massive Eiffel Tower greeting visitors at the entrance.

Never mind the tower: for the Chicago fair, an American engineer named George Washington Gale Ferris lent his name to a giant wheel that, for fifty cents, lifted passengers high above the Chicago skyline—higher even than the new Statue of Liberty—each of its cars larger than a Pullman rail coach. Atop the Ferris wheel, as if aloft in a hot air balloon, passengers viewed Lake Michigan and the White City, a futuristic "city beautiful" free of industrial grime (and horse droppings). Constructed of a white plaster-and-jute mix spread over lightweight wood frames, the neoclassical beaux arts architectural fantasyland was replete with fountains, statuary, colonnades, arches, domes, and waterways afloat with gondolas. At night, electrified by thousands of Edison's incandescent bulbs, it shone like "the most flawless . . . human creation," one guidebook pronounced, and a civil engineer declared that the wheel encircled the domes of the White City like a halo.

Nearby, the Midway Plaisance, "a broad promenade lined with sideshows," won crowds of enthusiasts, with devilish horns a more apt accessory than a halo. There were "Bedouins," a "fearsome (canvas) Hawaiian volcano," and "a village of genuine savages." Champion prizefighter "Gentleman" Jim Corbett gave demonstrations of how he had defeated the great John L. Sullivan (courtesy of a sponsor, Fleischman's Yeast). One genteel young man from New York relished eye-popping "dancing girls with bare stomachs who wiggled in what clergymen said was a most abandoned way, right before everybody." To slake its patrons' thirsts, the Midway offered cider pressed by Normandy maids in the French pavilion, and beer served in the Old Vienna *haus*. (Pabst Blue Ribbon won a prize.) But cocktails? The Columbian? The Ferris? The White City? None of the above. Nonetheless, one chronicler has unearthed a drink named for the "Windy City, long before bombs, machine guns and sawed-off shotguns" disturbed the peace.

Far from vaudeville and the world's fair, Chicago's perhaps most notorious "cocktail" was served to unsuspecting customers at the Lone Star Saloon and Palm Garden Restaurant. From 1896 to 1903, the manager there, Mickey Finn, was said to add "knockout drops" (chloral hydrate) to a patron's drink and relied upon his "house girls" to assist the unconscious patron into a rear room, then into a back alley that would provide an open-air accommodation for the night. Waking the next morning in the alley, the hapless Lone Star patron would find himself relieved of both his valuables and memory of the preceding night's events. The manager's name, however, lived in infamy, and the Mickey Finn became Chicago's most famous "mixed drink."

THE MAMIE TAYLOR

Ingredients

I ounce scotch whisky

Juice of ½ lime

Ginger ale

Ice

Directions

1. In tall glass, add 3–4 ice cubes.

2. Add scotch.

3. Add lime juice.

4. Fill to top with ginger ale, stir, and serve.

THE GIN FIZZ

Ingredients

I ounce gin

½ ounce lemon juice

¾ ounce clear syrup

I egg white

Ice cubes

Directions

1. Combine gin, lemon juice, syrup, and egg white in cocktail shaker.
2. Shake with vigor.
3. Add 3 or 4 ice cubes.
4. Shake vigorously.
5. Strain into glass, spritz with siphon, and serve.

THE CHICAGO

Ingredients

¾ ounce Jamaica rum

¾ ounce port wine

Juice of ¼ lemon

½ teaspoon sugar

White of I egg

Ice

Directions

1. Combine ingredients in shaker and shake vigorously.
2. Strain into tall glass with ice.
3. Fill to top with seltzer.

NEW ORLEANS

Though French explorers in 1718 pronounced their new set-
tlement La Nouvelle-Orléans, a sharp bend in the Mississippi

River earned the Gulf port city its nickname, the Crescent City. But another moniker, the Big Easy, garnered from an early 1900s nightspot of that name, better suited the temperament of the city known for its devotion to music, dance, and dining. In culinary terms, New Orleans cuisine resembled a repertoire of the dishes from Spain, France, Africa, the West Indies, Mexico, Cuba, and Atlantic Canada, its chefs and bartenders finding inspiration in a trove of herbs, spices, and other seasonings, from sugarcane to cayenne.

Visitors descended on the city regularly, especially for the annual, weeklong pre-Lenten revelry known as Mardi Gras (translation: Fat Tuesday), a prelude to Catholics' six weeks of penitential self-sacrifice in advance of Easter. Among the revelers in 1903 was Alice Roosevelt (b. 1884), the daughter of President Theodore Roosevelt and a houseguest of the McIlheney family, producers of the ubiquitous Tabasco sauce. "For a week," Alice recalled, "we went nearly every evening to a carnival ball," held at the French Opera House. Alice, an honored guest, played her part at the Mardi Gras court. "First, there was a tableau of the masks, then the 'queen' was brought down from her box, crowned, and seated beside the 'king' on their throne, and all the court danced around them. Then I was escorted from my box, paraded across the stage, given a parchment which welcomed me to the 'king' and 'queen,'" she wrote. "After that every one on the stage danced. . . . No one was supposed to know who the masks were," she explained, "their identity was supposed to be secret."

Alice Roosevelt made no secret of her preference for wines over spirits. ("I should never have thought of taking . . . whiskey or cocktails"), but in her two-week sojourn for Mardi Gras, the president's daughter surely dined with John McIlheney and his mother at Commander's Palace, a restaurant famed for its Creole seafood fare and for the city's signature cocktail, Planter's Punch. The Palace's Victorian architecture, with its turret and gingerbread trim, contrasted with the surrounding Greek Revival mansions with broad galleries in the prestigious Garden District, but the restaurant beckoned diners to an interior of mahogany moldings and Baccarat crystal chandeliers. Alice may have sipped "a glass of sherry, or madeira, of white wine or claret" as she wrote in her memoir, *Crowded Hours* (1933), while her companions most certainly enjoyed another of the city's signature cocktails: the Sazerac.

PLANTER'S PUNCH

Ingredients

> 1½ ounces light rum
> ½ ounce orange juice
> ½ ounce grapefruit juice
> ⅓ ounce grenadine
> ½ ounce dark rum
> Ice (cubed)

Directions

> 1. Fill goblet with ice.
> 2. Pour in juices and light rum.
> 3. Add grenadine.
> 4. Stir.
> 5. Add dark rum.

THE SAZERAC

Ingredients

> $1\frac{1}{2}$ ounces rye whiskey
>
> 1 dash Pernod or absinthe
>
> Few dashes Peychaud's bitters
>
> Few dashes Angostura bitters
>
> 1 dash Italian vermouth
>
> Ice chips

Directions

> 1. Chill an Old Fashioned glass.
> 2. Coat inside of glass with Pernod or absinthe.
> 3. In second glass, combine Italian vermouth, rye, and bitters.
> 4. Stir and strain into first (chilled) glass

SAN FRANCISCO

Touring California in 1890, the Bostonian Miss Susie Clark reserved the state's most "cosmopolitan" city for the finale of her travelogue, *The Round Trip* (1890). At "so magnificent a harbor as San Francisco Bay," she exclaimed, one could easily imagine all the "navies of the world" sheltered in its "commodious anchorage." She swooned at the "paradise" of Golden Gate Park, the "precipitous heights" of the hills, and the "magnificent" palatial "residences of the *elite*." She doubtless found time to admire the homes of four "railroad kings"—Collis Huntington, Leland Stanford, Charles Crocker, Mark Hopkins—who in 1869 had thrust the Central Pacific eastward over the Sierra range to join the Union Pacific, inaugurating the Transcontinental Railroad.

While the "kings" had exploited Chinese laborers and the gullibility of the Congress to win favorable contracts, in recent years their San Francisco palaces had risen atop Nob Hill to grace the "etherealized air." The "richness of the city and the lavish display of its wealth cannot fail to impress the visitor," Miss Clark continued, remarking, nonetheless, on the "noisy, tumultuous" atmosphere, the "cable-cars with clanging alarm-bells whizzing by." Her travelogue darkened with the remark that "observance of the Sabbath is quite an obsolete custom" in San Francisco, "perhaps because of the foreign mixture in the population."

The "mixture" had started with the "Spanish regime" of Mexicans and the Spanish padres who zealously "Christianized" native tribes into "submission." The city's newer Chinatown, which previously had been extoled by an East Coast visitor as "safe and orderly," horrified Miss Clark as an "ulcer gnawing at the city's heart," so repellent that the lady retired her pen before describing San Francisco's waterfront scene, named for the North African pirate coast. Frequented by sailors, San Francisco's Barbary Coast meant saloons: the Bowhead, the Grizzly Bear, the Whale, and others irresistible to mariners who were "free spenders and not over-captious about the quality of the liquor served them." The popular Cowboy's Rest, ruled by the voluptuous blonde Maggie Kelly, the Queen of the Barbary Coast, combined the saloon with a rooming house. ("Whoever rented one of her rooms was never asked any embarrassing questions.")

While the Golden State's vineyards flourished, the grape in high demand was reportedly the "Italia or La Rosa del Peru, named for the Peruvian port from which it was shipped." Chile also claimed the grape, but, South American rivalry aside, the brandy it yielded, known as "pisco," most probably had traveled north to San Francisco by way of the 1849 gold rush that lured prospectors from Australia, Europe, and Latin America. By the 1870s, pisco brandy was shipped to San Francisco "in earthen jars, broad at the top and tapering down to a point, holding about five gallons each." Ship's officers and the city's businessmen avoided Barbary Coast saloons in favor of gentlemanly establishments where they imbibed San Francisco's signature cocktail, Pisco Punch.

At the Bank Exchange on Montgomery Street, "a magnificently appointed saloon paved with marble and decorated with oil paintings valued at a hundred thousand dollars," the bartender, Duncan Nichol, delighted patrons with his secret recipe for punch mixed with pisco, the brandy revered by one chronicler as "perfectly colourless, quite fragrant, very seductive, terribly strong . . . with a flavor somewhat resembling that of scotch whisky, but much more delicate, with a marked fruity taste." The Pisco Punch was served, he recalled, "hot, with a bit of lemon and a dash of nutmeg in it." The first glass, he said, "satisfied me that San Francisco was, and is, a nice place to visit." Imbibing the second glass, he felt he "could face small-pox, all the fevers known . . . and the Asiatic cholera, combined, if need be."

On April 18, 1906, San Franciscans awoke with sharp tremors at dawn, perhaps fearing the previous night's overindulgence in pisco—only to find all San Francisco shaking from a major earthquake. "Suddenly the earth began to heave, with a sickening onrush of motions," wrote Jack London's wife, Charmian. Flames ravaged the city, buildings collapsed, and San Franciscans fled on foot, many dragging trunks or valises hastily stuffed with belongings. With nearly 80 percent of the city destroyed, recovery seemed a far-off prospect.

San Francisco, however, rose to the challenge: on July 23, three months after the catastrophe, the Saint Francis Hotel reopened, proclaiming service in the "FIRST MENU IN THE NEW HOTEL AFTER THE EARTHQUAKE AND FIRE OF 1906." The featured beverage: The St. Francis cocktail.

PISCO PUNCH

Ingredients

> 2 ounces pisco
>
> I ounce pineapple juice
>
> ¾ ounce lemon juice
>
> Ice
>
> Lemon twist

Directions

> 1. Combine pisco and juices.
> 2. Shake with ice.
> 3. Strain into glass.
> 4. Garnish with lemon twist.

THE ST. FRANCIS

Ingredients

> 2–3 ounces gin
>
> I dash dry vermouth
>
> I dash orange bitters
>
> Ice

Directions

> 1. Add ice to mixing glass or shaker.
> 2. Pour in gin.
> 3. Add vermouth and bitters.
> 4. Stir and strain into chilled cocktail glass.

Oh, the Places They Toast!

Sentiment swelled at the mahogany bars over drinks that recalled a faraway childhood home or, perhaps, a beloved friend's location, or the place where a great fortune was quarried, milled, dammed, herded, mined, or cut and floated to a sawmill. Whichever it might have been, the place names for specialty cocktails mapped the Gilded Age from Newport to Florida, Montauk to Hawaii.

NEWPORT

> Avoid Newport like the plague until you are certain that you
> will be accepted there. If you don't, it will be your Waterloo.
> ～ Henry Symes Lehr

The shocking defeat of the invincible Napoleon Bonaparte at the Battle of Waterloo in 1815 echoed into the Gilded Age, when skirmishes for social standing rivaled the most complex military campaigns. The new battleground was Newport, Rhode Island, and the stakes couldn't be higher.

No one knew this better than Harry Lehr (b. 1869), the social arbiter who started adult life as an impecunious champagne salesman but endeared himself to Mrs. Astor, the "Queen" of New York Society, and to her circle of prominent women friends. The crafty Lehr then courted a vulnerable but enormously wealthy young widow, Elizabeth Drexel Dahlgren, married her, and pursued a life as Society's own court jester, ever ready to turn idle hours into amusement for the bored rich.

The late 1800s Gilded Age brought the wealthy potentates of Gotham to the rocky spit of land once known as Aquidneck Island, where Newport, the summertime kingdom of "King" Lehr, became the "nation's social capital." For six weeks annually, July through August, spectacular house parties and yachting events filled the calendar, complementing the tennis tournament, the polo match, and the horse show that closed the season. Cool, breezy Newport had long been a summertime retreat for wealthy Southerners fleeing their steamy rice and cotton plantations, along with New Englanders who enjoyed the change of

scenery. Now the moneyed newcomers anchored their yachts in the harbor and built mansion-sized, seafront "cottages" they christened with stately names touched with charm: the Breakers, the Elms, Beechwood, and Marble House.

"The regular afternoon diversion at Newport," recalled the bestselling and socially prominent author Edith Wharton, "was a drive. All the elderly ladies, leaning back in Victoria or Barouche . . . drove the whole length of Bellevue Avenue, where the most fashionable villas stood, and the newly laid-out Ocean Drive." "For the drive," as with most public events, "it was necessary to dress . . . elegantly." The social whirl, however, was accompanied by the frisson of danger. Mrs. Harry Lehr dubbed Newport "the playground of the great ones of the earth from which all intruders were ruthlessly excluded by a set of cast-iron rules." Woe unto social aspirants who found themselves ostracized as mere interlopers, invisible although in plain sight.

The Newport season flowed with champagne, while its signature cocktail was more likely favored elsewhere in the off-season, when the imbiber thirsted for Newport at its summertime best.

NEWPORT COCKTAIL

Ingredients

> 1 ounce Gordon's gin
> 1 ounce French vermouth
> ½ ounce Italian vermouth
> Orange peel

Directions

1. In mixing glass with ice, add gin.
2. Add both vermouths.
3. Stir, strain, and pour into cocktail glass.
4. Squeeze and add orange peel, and serve.

MONTAUK

In his mind's eye, poet Walt Whitman spanned the world with an imagination as expansive as America in the Gilded Age. Gazing seaward, he penned "From Montauk Point" (1888–89) from the eastern end of Long Island, thought of as "the Western terminus of transatlantic steamship lines."

> I stand as on some mighty eagle's beak,
> Eastward the sea absorbing, viewing, (nothing but sea
>   and sky,)
> The tossing waves, the foam, the ships in the distance,
> The wild unrest, the snowy, curling caps—that
>   inbound urge
> and urge of waves,
> Seeking the shores forever.

Though the poet expressed ambivalence toward alcohol, especially as the temperance movement seethed, others tippled in tribute to Montauk Point.

MONTAUK COCKTAIL

Ingredients

- 1 ounce gin
- 1 ounce French vermouth
- 1 ounce Italian vermouth
- 2 dashes Peychaud's bitters

Directions

1. In Old Fashioned glass with ice, combine gin and both French and Italian vermouth.
2. Add bitters.
3. Stir and serve.

FLORIDA

Swamps and alligators fueled the old legends of Florida, but new and easy escapes from winter branded its peninsular east coast the "American Riviera." Thanks to the entrepreneurial Henry Morrison Flagler (b. 1830), a founder of Standard Oil and restless Gilded Age tycoon, by 1904 the Florida East Coast Railway ferried sun seekers southward along the Eastern seaboard from New York to Jacksonville, Saint Augustine, Palm Beach, and Biscayne Bay. Flagler's passengers, dining behind plate glass windows in the train's elegant Pullman cars, watched the snowy scenes recede and the Carolina pines give way to Florida palms. A few might have fanned the pages of *Baedeker's Florida*, which the German travel publishing company had debuted in 1904, putting Florida on the international map, so to speak, while others preferred to socialize while looking forward to weeks-long stays in one of Mr. Flagler's luxurious hotels.

It had been noticed by the historian of the period, Justin Kaplan, that "men who have become rich in the States" showed a "propensity" to build hotels that matched "the largeness of American ideas." Flagler planted the flag of his own hotel empire in St. Augustine, where he constructed the palatial Ponce De Leon Hotel, which opened in 1888, and then hacked through the marsh to construct his thousand-room Royal Poinciana Hotel in Palm Beach, and two years later the Palm Beach Inn, renamed the Breakers in 1901.

In 1906, the famed expatriate author Henry James (b. 1863) made the rail trip to Florida on a lecture tour, while compiling an account of his travels that would be published in 1907 as *The American Scene*. The self-styled "pilgrim" was reacquainting himself with the America he had left twenty years earlier to take up residence in England. While his native New England had retained its charms, James was rattled by the noisy, outsized industrial-era New York City, whose "harsh winter" prompted an acquaintance at the Waldorf-Astoria Hotel to suggest James might enjoy a stay in tropical Florida. Taking copious notes, the literary traveler immersed himself in the luxe "hotel world" of the Breakers. "The sky, the sunset, the orange, the pineapple, the palm . . . the divine bougainvillea," all were a vivid contrast to descriptions of the swamps and "rank vegetation" he remembered from boyhood adventure novels.

James's meditation on Florida made no mention of Henry Flagler, the Gilded Age conquistador, but Flagler himself determined to extend his railroad in the years ahead to Florida's farmost island, Key West, nicknamed America's Gibraltar. The rail tycoon rode the first train on the Florida Overseas Railroad to Key West 1912, and died the following year. A category five hurricane irreparably damaged the overseas rail line in 1935, crushing Flagler's dreams like those of the Spanish explorers in their futile search for the city of El Dorado, centuries before. The Florida cocktail, a simple affair, pays sweet tribute to the fruit whose succulence aided and abetted the idea of tropical pleasures.

FLORIDA COCKTAIL

Ingredients

Orange juice

Italian vermouth

Directions

1. In tall (Collins) glass with ice cubes, add desired amount of strained juice.
2. Add vermouth equal to amount of juice.
3. Stir and serve.

HAWAII

From the deck of the ship *Ajax* in March 1866, the young American journalist Samuel Clemens glimpsed the Sandwich Islands, a sight that would thrill visitors who later arrived in Hawaii by ocean liner and, much later, by air. Named for the Fourth Earl of Sandwich by the British captain James Cook, who had explored the archipelago in 1778, the chain of volcanic islands in the North Pacific maintained their native names: Oahu, Kauai. Nihau, Molokai, Maui, Lanai, Kahoolawe, and the biggest one of all, Hawaii, on which an active volcano periodically slathered hillsides with molten lava and sent thunderheads of smoke and ash skyward in the name of the goddess Pele. "As we approached," he observed, "Diamond Head rose up out of the ocean."

Clemens, writing as Mark Twain, had come to compose a series of semi-satirical travel letters about the islands, having earned his stripes as a reporter for the *Territorial Enterprise* in Nevada. He would also sketch the history of the island kingdom, when Kamehameha the Great ("a sort of a Napoleon in military genius") defeated rival island chiefs and from 1810 ruled the unified islands with a tight hierarchy of taboos, rules, and regulations. The Christian missionaries' arrival in the 1820s from New England's ports heralded vast change, for the Hawaiians were thereafter clothed, churched, and "civilized" in the classically prudent style of New England.

Such men and women, Twain acknowledged, "had braved a thousand privations" en route to Hawaii, only to impose an industrial economic work ethic on nature's paradise. The missionaries, Twain wrote, showed "what rapture it is to work all day long for fifty cents to buy food for the next day, compared with fishing for a pastime and lolling in the shade through eternal summer, and eating of the bounty that nobody labored to provide but Nature. How sad it is," Twain concluded, "to think of the multitudes who have gone to their graves in this beautiful island and never knew there was a hell."

Much had changed several decades later when Alice Roosevelt, the president's daughter, sailed aboard the SS *Manchuria* from San Francisco in 1905 as part of a congressional "good will" delegation bound for the Far East. The first stop: "the island of Oahu in the early dawn light, mountains and valleys in cloudy green down to the line of the white beach." Now an American territory, Honolulu had been the capital city of the island nation since it was annexed by the United States in 1898.

The intervening seven years had not dimmed Hawaiians' resentment that a US-supported coup had resulted in the adoption of the "Bayonet Constitution" and that their king, David Kal kaua, had been reduced to mere ceremonial status in Washington. After his death, his sister, Queen Liliʻuokalani, had been arrested, tried for treason, and imprisoned over her attempt to restore the powers of the monarchy. The Kanakas—the Polynesian native peoples—knew their land had been usurped by traders, by Christian missionaries, and especially by the missionaries' adult children, the industrial corporate "sugar barons" who now ruled Hawaii with the backing of the White House, the Congress, and the US Navy.

The visiting congressional delegation thought nothing of this recent unpleasantness when the party sailed from the Golden Gate into cerulean Pacific waters, saw schools of flying fish, and, reaching Honolulu, heard "Hawaiian tunes and ukuleles" sung and played by "natives who came out to meet the steamer." "The entire population seemed to be on the wharf to meet us," Alice remarked, "and garland us with leis of heavy, perfumed flowers, gardenias, and ginger blossoms." The president's daughter lunched at the original Royal Hawaiian Hotel, toured a sugar plantation, and took a lesson in dancing the hula. An afternoon of "swimming and surf-boating" on a Waikiki beach prompted Alice to speak for generations of future visitors who, adorned with flower necklaces (leis), lamented upon departure: "I did not want to leave."

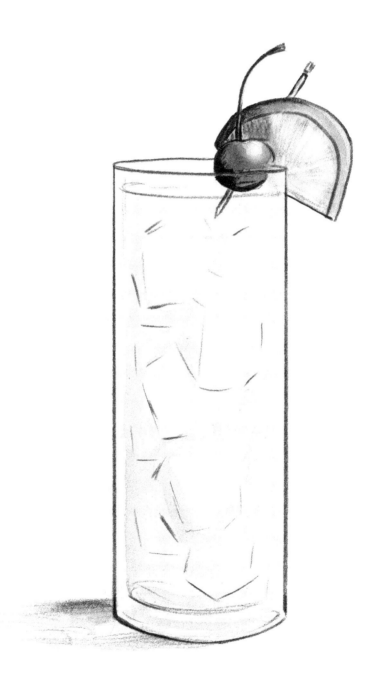

HAWAII COCKTAIL

Ingredients

1½ ounces whiskey (bourbon or rye)

Juice of 1 orange

Peel of entire orange

Ginger ale

Ice

Directions

1. Put ice and orange peel in tall Collins glass.
2. Add whiskey.
3. Add juice.
4. Stir.
5. Top with ginger ale, stir gently, and serve.

HONOLULU COCKTAIL

Ingredients

1½ ounces Tom gin

1 teaspoon lime juice

1 teaspoon orange juice

2 dashes Angostura bitters

Twist of lemon peel

Directions

1. In mixing glass with ice, add gin.
2. Add juices.
3. Add bitters.
4. Stir, strain, and serve with lemon twist on top.

KLONDIKE

Yukon! Klondike!—words that burst with blinding visions of wealth to rival any others in the Gilded Age. Jack London, at twenty-one years of age, answered the call when the discovery of gold in Canada's northland in 1897 launched a gold rush the equal of the California fever of 1849. According to *Appleton's Canadian Guide-Book* of 1899, in the preceding year "an immense tide of gold seekers, estimated at from 20,000 to 30,000, poured into the Klondike, and the output of the mines for the year was placed at about $10,000,000." Prospectors stampeded northward, and the hunt was on.

But where, exactly, were the Yukon goldfields? Appleton's located them in "the Northwest Territories of Canada . . . a vast stretch of country lying between the Arctic Ocean on the North, the 141st west meridian or international boundary which separates it from the Territory of Alaska." His chapter "How to Reach the Gold Fields" advised a steamer from Seattle or Vancouver to Skagway. The next stops along the way were the boomtowns where Klondikers bought grubstake supplies and caught their breath: Dyea, Dawson, Fort Selkirk.

And then, the Chilkoot Pass. The steep icy summit at the boundary between Alaska and Canada, at an elevation of over three thousand feet, posed the first great test. Horses or other pack animals proved useless, so the pass had to be climbed and crossed on foot, each prospector his own "beast of burden," pulling a sled and harnessed into a backpack. Many turned back in defeat. Others, ill-equipped, continued at their peril and lost life's gamble before Canada's North-West Mounted Police established a checkpoint at the peak. The Mounties allowed prospectors to proceed into the punishing terrain and subzero winter weather only if each individual packed in a ton of gear and provisions—including 150 pounds of bacon, 400 of flour, 125 of dried beans, and 10 of coffee and tea, along with picks and shovels, wool mittens, saw, rope, tent, matches, and other items—estimated to sustain life for a year.

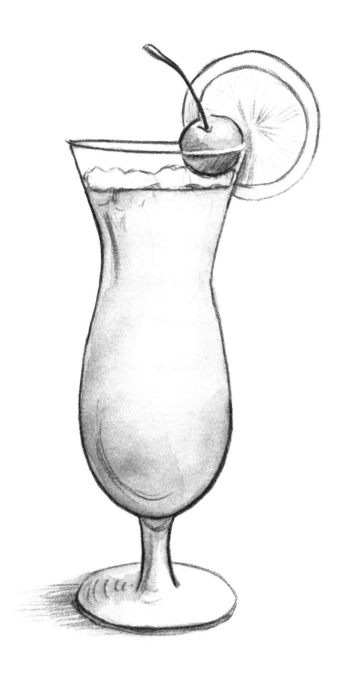

A few found fortunes, though most did not. The guide teased readers who might be mulling over the odds for themselves: "The wealth of the Klondike can, as yet, only be conjectured, but experienced miners, familiar with the richest properties of America and the world, confidently predict that the new Eldorado will produce annually at least $10,000,000 for many years to come." The Klondike cocktail could celebrate a strike—or, at least, a gold field miner's survival.

KLONDIKE COCKTAIL

Ingredients

> 1½ ounces whiskey
>
> Juice of 1 orange
>
> Peel of entire orange
>
> Ice
>
> Ginger ale

Directions

> 1. In Collins glass with ice, add orange peel.
> 2. Add whiskey.
> 3. Add juice.
> 4. Stir moderately.
> 5. Fill to top with ginger ale and serve.

❧ 7 ❧

Quaffing Collegians

In the decades following the Civil War, the young gentlemen from the nation's elite preparatory schools arrived. Along the brick sidewalks of sedate Cambridge, Massachusetts, down the streets of New Haven, Connecticut, and the providential Providence, Rhode Island, as well as to Princeton, New Jersey, and over the gorges of upstate Ithaca, New York. They came from St. Paul's and St. Mark's, from Groton, and, for a few, from a rigid European *gymnasium* or a home schoolroom where tutors held sway.

For many young men of privilege, college life meant a suite that was faithfully serviced by a "scout" (valet and servant), who also tidied his gentleman's lodgings and kept coal or wood supplied for his fireplace in chilly weather, setting the fires and clearing the ashes as needed. The "scout" also tended the collegian's wardrobe, which ran the gamut from tweeds to tuxedos, his hats from straw to felt to beaver. Eschewing the dining "commons," the young gentlemen often preferred to take meals in the private eating clubs.

Athletics and fitness mattered greatly during the college semesters, including horsemanship for those who stabled a saddle horse near the campus and perhaps shipped a pony cart for amusing outings in the vicinity. (If so, a man must keep an eye on his groom or liveryman, careful that his horse was well fed and brushed, the tack cleaned and burnished.) Otherwise, according to one observer, his *de rigueur* sporting goods included "tennis-rackets, canoe paddles, golf-clubs, and polo-sticks." Beyond racket sports, the boxing gloves beckoned, or perhaps the crewman's oars, the dumbbells at the gymnasium, or, possibly, the pigskin on the football gridiron. (If not "rooting" in the grandstand during the fall season, a man might cheerlead with a megaphone from the sidelines). Skiing and ice-skating were appropriate in season, and casual baseball when the weather warmed.

Loyalty and tradition endured. The bas-relief school insignia was cast on cufflinks, the school colors woven into neckties and mufflers, and pennants adorned the students' walls—the Harvard crimson, the Yale blue, Brown's brown and red, the orange and black of Princeton, Cornell's solid red. No less distinctive was the campus's signature drink, shaken or blended in homage to a venerable school and its alumni. Years after the sheepskin was awarded (and ever afterward in the rosy glow of reverie), the college cocktail reminded an old grad of his youthful days. (The gentleman's "C" on the academic transcript was perfectly acceptable.)

HARVARD

For a certain set of Harvard fellows, who crossed the Charles to imbibe along Bowdoin Square in Boston's West End, the Shandygaff cocktail was the libation of choice. Young Theodore Roosevelt (b. 1858) perhaps joined his classmates for many a Shandygaff evening, for his biographer, Edmund Morris, observes that he "caroused with his friends" in "time-honored undergraduate fashion." As a Harvard College freshman, Roosevelt described a typical school day in a letter to his mother, "Mittie" (Martha Bulloch Roosevelt), a missive that would appear in the first of eight published volumes of his letters. The account provides a template of the gentleman's experience of Harvard that obscured the very hard study pursued by the future president and his classmates. "Teddy" Roosevelt portrayed the college man as he might wish to be seen, a figure of boastful insouciance.

In September 1876, "Freshman" Roosevelt was comfortably ensconced in a boardinghouse midway between Harvard Yard and the Charles. His lodgings were "tastefully papered, the carpet deep and warm," and his chaise longue was cushioned with pillows and a fur rug. His day began at "half past seven," when his "scout" called him from his slumbers, having "made the fire and blacked the boots." Breakfast consisted of "hot biscuits, toast, chops or beef steak, buckwheat cakes," and tea or coffee. The young man studied until 10:00 a.m., inspected his mail, then attended a recitation in Latin presided over by a "meek-eyed" professor, afterward venturing to the Hemenway gymnasium. ("I have a set-to with the gloves . . . for I am training to box among the light-weights in the approaching match for the championship of Harvard.")

His memorable lunch became an "obstreperously joyous" occasion, a food fight involving "a dutch cheese" (probably an entire waxed Gouda) and "dire threats of expulsion," which nonetheless segued into a placid, contemplative afternoon devoted to study and the "recitation" that preceded a "pleasant, home-like" dinner. Closing the day, Roosevelt "studied for an hour," and then, by ten thirty, he "put on his slippers," drew the rocking chair up to the fire, and spent the next half-hour reading and "toasting" his feet. His biographer adds that the fall season found Roosevelt enjoying "matinees, theater parties, and balls."

THE SHANDYGAFF

Ingredients

½ pint English bitter or pub ale of choice

½ pint ginger beer

Instructions

1. Fill a pint glass or stein halfway with the beer.
2. Fill the rest of the way with the ginger beer.

THE HARVARD COCKTAIL

Ingredients

$3/5$ jigger brandy

$3/5$ jigger Italian vermouth

1 dash orange bitters

Cracked ice

Directions

1. In shaker, combine brandy and vermouth.
2. Stir.
3. Add orange bitters.
4. Add ice.
5. Shake and spritz with siphon.

YALE

Founded by Puritan ministers in 1701 as a theological seminary, by 1716 Collegiate College had been renamed after an endowment by Elihu Yale, governor of the British East Indian Company. As the Gilded Age dawned, it had long educated the men who were meant to hold the reins of economic authority

in the nation. Wall Street and the banks would be theirs by
secular and divine right.

The Yale College motto, *Lux et Veritas* (Latin for "light and
truth"), must have tolled with keen irony for freshman Clarence Day, Jr. (b. 1874), son of the New York railroad financier
Clarence Day, Sr., as his first semester in New Haven drew
to a close. The future author of the bestselling *Life with Father*
(1935), young Clarence took stock of his first year's college
expenditures and found himself shamefully sunk in debt. He
owed his dormitory for seven weeks' board, his haberdasher
for "ascot ties and shirts and a pair of pointy-toed shoes," and
a tobacconist for "fancy pipes," including "a meerschaum head
of a bull with large amber horns." "There would be no more
money coming to me," he confessed, "until college opened
again in September."

Soon enough came the reckoning in Father's office at 38
Wall Street, where the senior Day asked:

"What about your allowance?"

"I'm sorry to say I've spent it all, Father."

"That was very imprudent of you," Father replied.

He evidently did not confess to his father (let alone to
Mother) that among his creditors was "Heublein's for rounds
of drinks I had signed for, on what had once seemed jolly
nights." At the West Hartford hotel restaurant they operated,
Gilbert and Louis Heublein had been perfecting a recipe for
premixed cocktails—the favorites were the Manhattan and
the Martini—which they would soon be shipping nationwide,
sparing the host the embarrassment of mixological impreci-
sion. Clarence no doubt enjoyed both and a penitential summer followed, with the young man working diligently as an
office boy in Father's firm.

In his coming-of-age novel, *Stover at Yale* (1911), author Owen Johnson (Yale, class of 1900) introduces the young Dink Stover, who, like Clarence, outspends his allowance at the haberdasher's, where an irresistible green shirt multiplies into a panoply of shirts, collars, and silk socks, all charged to a newly opened account. Dink also spends freely at Mory's, the eatery that was synonymous with undergraduate life at Yale. "Make it two for me," Dink opens a drinking challenge at the popular oasis, vowing to match a classmate cocktail for cocktail until he loses count. When Mory's closes, Dink stumbles his way in darkness to his rooms and to bed where "the fog closed over his consciousness . . . and he was asleep." The reader may infer the name of Dink's drinks, but surely young Stover demanded the school's signature beverage, which calls for Tom gin, lighter than London dry on the juniper berry tang.

THE MARTINI

Ingredients

> 1½ ounces gin
>
> ½ teaspoon dry vermouth (or to taste)
>
> 1 green olive (not pitted)
>
> Ice cubes

Directions

> 1. Fill mixing glass with ice cubes.
> 2. Add gin.
> 3. Add vermouth.
> 4. Stir.
> 5. Strain into chilled martini glass.
> 6. Add olive and serve.

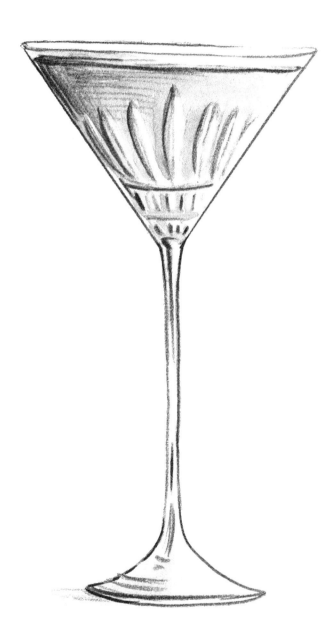

THE YALE COCKTAIL

Ingredients

1½ ounces Tom gin (chilled)

1½ ounces Italian vermouth

1 dash orange bitters

Seltzer water

Directions

1. Mix gin and vermouth in a short highball glass.
2. Add orange bitters.
3. Stir.
4. Top with spritz of seltzer.

BROWN

The American Revolution was fourteen years in the future when, in 1761, a merchant, a clerk-scribe, and a Congregationalist minister in Newport, Rhode Island, petitioned the colonial General Assembly to open "a literary institution or School for instructing young Gentlemen." The curriculum would feature "Languages, Mathematics, Geography & History, & such other branches of Knowledge as shall be desired." The campus, the three understood, must include "a public Building or Buildings for the boarding of the youth & the Residence of the Professors." Messrs. Josias Lyndon and William Ellery, Jr., and the Reverend Ezra Stiles thus launched the institution that became Brown University, once the school was relocated to Providence with the financial support of the mercantile Brown family—Nicholas, Nicholas Jr., John, Joseph, and Moses. (Joseph became a professor of natural philosophy at the college, and John and Nicholas Jr. served successively as treasurers from 1775 to 1825.)

The college accepted students regardless of religious affiliation, perhaps in the spirit of the colony's founder Roger Williams, an advocate for religious freedom. By the late 1800s, however, Brown University was loosely affiliated with the Baptist Church—spiritual home of Standard Oil titan John D. Rockefeller, a lifelong teetotaler. The senior Rockefeller's namesake, John D. Junior, a nondrinker like his father, attended Brown (class of 1897), where he sang in the glee club, played the mandolin, became junior class president, won a Phil Beta Kappa key, and, like the senior Rockefeller, reportedly watched every penny. A member of the Baptist Church, John D. Junior also taught a Bible class while at Brown. Though he no doubt would have called his students' attention to cautionary verses about the perils of drink, like the other Ivies his alma mater celebrated a signature cocktail.

THE BROWN COCKTAIL

Ingredients

> 1 ounce bourbon
>
> 1 ounce French vermouth
>
> 2 dashes orange bitters
>
> Ice

Directions

> 1. Combine whiskey and vermouth in ice-filled shaker.
> 2. Add bitters.
> 3. Stir and strain into chilled glass.

CORNELL

"Far above Cayuga's waters. . . ." goes the anthem chorused reverently by the sons and daughters of Cornell University, one of the nation's many colleges founded in the wake of the Morrill Land-Grant Act of 1862. Passed by Congress and signed into law by President Abraham Lincoln at the nadir of the Civil War, the legislation specified that each state of the Union establish an institution specializing in "agriculture and the mechanic arts. . . . without excluding other scientific and classical studies." Three years on, when the New York State Senate authorized its founding, a wealthy businessman and entrepreneur named Ezra Cornell donated his farmland in upstate Ithaca (and $500,000) to establish the state's official land grant institution.

The far-sighted Cornell also advised that women be educated at his namesake university and by 1870 women had entered the classrooms there to earn baccalaureate degrees. Among Cornell's Gilded Age pioneers were the feminist and social activist Florence Kelley (b. 1859) and botanist Liberty Hyde Bailey (b. 1858). Kelley's senior thesis examining the history of children's status under the law formed the basis of her years-long commitment to spotlight the plight of the nation's children, especially underage workers in mills and factories, and to push for laws advancing social justice. After she received her bachelor of arts degree in 1882, she would eventually earn a law degree from Chicago's Northwestern University at night and become a resident at Jane Addams's Hull-House in Chicago, where Addams's nephew, who saw her "fixed resolution" at close range, remarked on her determination "to make the salvation of women and children from blind industrial greed the work of her life."

For his part, Bailey joined the faculty in 1888 to chair the Department of Practical and Experimental Horticulture and would go on to edit the *Cyclopedia of American Horticulture* (1900–2) and *Cyclopedia of American Agriculture* (1907–9), earning him fellowship in the American Association of Arts and Sciences.

Whether their careers took them into horticulture, engineering, or other fields, Cornell graduates were said to toast their alma mater with the Cornell.

THE CORNELL COCKTAIL

Ingredients

1½ ounces Gordon's gin (chilled if possible)

1½ ounces French vermouth

Ice (optional)

Directions

1. Mix gin and vermouth.
2. Stir.
3. Ice may be added if desired.

PRINCETON

Founded in 1746 as the College of New Jersey, Princeton was initially the seat of theological study for the Scottish-Irish Presbyterian ministry. The storied Nassau Hall became the center of Princeton student life by 1756, and the American Revolution left a cannonball bruise from the Battle of Princeton (and qualified "Old Nassau" for historical landmark status).

Though Princeton did not discriminate among denominations, Presbyterian doctrine stamped the school well into the Gilded Age under President James McCosh, who also promoted ideas of "divinely sanctioned rights to wealth, property, and freedom from interference by government." Through two presidential decades (1868–88), McCosh assured the young men of Princeton that the "hand of God" guided human endeavors in quest of "wealth," and the largesse of the steel manufacturer Andrew Carnegie apparently proved the point. The philanthropist's donation to the university dammed the Millstone River—and voilà—Lake Carnegie was created, newly placid waters for the Princeton oarsmen.

From the Princeton student body in this era emerged the proponent of a profession new to the Gilded Age that flourishes to this day. Since boyhood in post–Civil War Atlanta, Ivy Ledbetter Lee (b. 1877) heard the voices of civic leaders in the family parsonage as his father, a "silver-tongued" Protestant minister, elegantly fused scripture with diplomacy. As a collegian, Lee transferred from Emory to Princeton, where he wrote for the *Daily Princetonian* and pondered a career in journalism (law school seeming prohibitively expensive). After graduation, he worked as a reporter for the *New York Times* and spent a few months working as publicist for a New York mayoral candidate. Lee then opened an office at 20 Broad Street (adjacent to the stock exchange), barely meeting expenses as a press agent for politicians, an insurance heir, and a circus.

Blessed with the "lean physique and carriage of an ambitious man," Lee seized the opportunity during a 1902 coal strike to reverse the usual corporate custom of secrecy, which had roused the public's suspicion of big business. Instead, Lee promoted "transparency" and the idea that corporations, like people, had stories to tell. Soon enough, Ivy Lee & Associates was ensconced in a Manhattan high-rise suite of offices, busily narrating compelling sagas for clients that included railroads; tobacco, steel, rubber, and meatpacking firms; banks; and public utilities. Though he imbibed Apollinaris and other mineral waters, Lee necessarily socialized with the New York businessmen over cocktails.

THE PRINCETON COCKTAIL

Ingredients

⅔ jigger Tom gin (chilled)

1 dash orange bitters

Seltzer water (chilled)

Directions

1. Pour gin into highball glass.
2. Add bitters.
3. Stir.
4. Fill with seltzer.

❧ 8 ❧

Bubbles

The serious business of effervescence flowed through mineral waters, soda, and seltzer, but discerning ladies and gentlemen awaited the moment when the cork popped from a bottle of chilled champagne. The tap water of the well-to-do, champagne was poured by the magnum in the Gilded Age at private parties, balls, certain sporting events, and at Society's favorite restaurants, such as Delmonico's, Sherry's, or the Waldorf dining room. Stowed in the hold of a ship or yacht, or a well-stocked cellar in townhouse or country estate, the fermented French champagne grape served its enlivening purpose in all seasons, a *sine qua non*—the thing absolutely necessary.

Vintage and vintner mattered. The social arbiter of the era, Ward McAllister (b. 1827), tucked an entire champagne advisory into his manual of social climbing, *Society as I Have Found It* (1890). "Champagne and Other Wines" steered Society to the perfect bubbly in a crystal flute. "It will be well to remember that champagnes are now known to *connoisseurs* by their vintage," McAllister insisted. "In keeping champagnes, keep only . . . the best." The risk of mistaking the ordinary for the "best" was well worth the gamble, but the necessity clear: "to possess something that no one else has."

In his guide, McAllister painstakingly described the chilling of the bottle, as if his compatriots might not have mastered the technique "to properly *frappé* champagne." Into a champagne bucket ("a pail"), "small pieces of ice" were to be layered with rock salt, and the bottle carefully inserted "to keep the neck free from the ice." If possible, "turn the bottle every five minutes. . . . In twenty-five minutes, it should be in perfect condition, and should be served immediately." The proof was in the pouring: "for one who likes it cold, the wine should be cooled sufficiently to form a bead on the outside of the glass into which it is poured. It is pretty, and the perfection of condition."

THE CHAMPAGNE COCKTAIL

Ingredients

Chilled champagne

1 lump sugar

2 dashes Angostura bitters

1 piece of lemon peel, twisted

Directions

1. In champagne glass, add sugar and bitters.

2. Fill glass with champagne.

3. Add lemon twist.

⌖ 9 ⌖

"Demon Rum"

One veteran bartender, A. William Schmidt, admitted that "it may sound strange from the lips of a mixer of drinks, but still it is the truth—*I believe in temperance*." Years behind the bar had taught Schmidt the difference between those who appreciated "artistically mixed drinks" and those who, enslaved to alcohol, craved the strongest liquor to quickly reach a "nirvana" of inebriation. Two bestselling writers of the era, Jack London and reforming journalist Jacob Riis, amplified Schmidt's caveat and weighed in on the side of temperance, London in his memoir *John Barleycorn* (1913), and Riis in his muckraking exposé *How the Other Half Lives* (1890). Riis vehemently denounced the "Reign of Rum" in which saloons cast their "colossal shadow," an "omen of evil" darkening public life in New York and elsewhere.

A third marquee writer of the period, Upton Sinclair (b. 1878), decried the crisis both in memoir and fiction. The son of a Baltimore whiskey salesman, he observed that his father's average workday began innocently with "lemonade or ginger-ale," but arced toward whiskey by nightfall, often to celebrate a happily concluded business "deal." The routine became the senior Sinclair's undoing and the despair of his wife and young son, who learned that the drinks thrilling to the palettes of the multitudes—"mint juleps, toddies, hot Scotches, egg-nogs, punch"—were calamitous to those who imbibed at their peril. Whiskey was boyhood's gauntlet for young Sinclair, who swore that mixed drinks constituted his boyhood's "most conspicuous single fact."

Sinclair diagnosed his father's affliction in two words that would be familiar to most Americans: "demon rum." Years later, Sinclair authored *The Jungle* (1907), a blockbuster novel that exposed impurities in Americans' leading brand-name breakfast meats. Horrified by the novel's revelations of the packing industry's brutal standards and tainted products, Sinclair's readers overlooked the pro-temperance messages stitched into numerous scenes of drunkenness, in which alcohol lay waste to rich and poor alike. The bestselling Sinclair readily proclaimed himself a vegetarian and a teetotaler.

Sinclair's demonic rum nonetheless warmed those for whom hot rum libations proved irresistible on many a wintry night.

HOT SPICED RUM

Ingredients

> 2 ounces dark rum
> 1 sugar cube
> 1 teaspoon ground cloves
> 4 ounces hot water
> Nutmeg (optional)

Directions

1. Combine rum, sugar, and cloves in warmed cup or mug.
2. Add hot water and stir.
3. If desired, grate nutmeg on top.

"JOHN BARLEYCORN"

"One afternoon," recalled the teenage Adela Rogers (b. 1894), who would gain fame as a writer in the Gilded Age and well beyond (and was the model for *Brenda Starr, Girl Reporter*), her father and Jack London "took off down the road to visit some of Jack's cronies," promising "to be home early." At the time, father and daughter were guests of Jack and Charmian London at their ranch in Glen Ellen in Northern California's Sonoma Valley, where they enjoyed horseback riding, swimming in the Londons' spring-fed lake, and convivial evenings that began with cocktails and proceeded to dinner where wine flowed freely. Conversation ranged widely and seriously between Adela's adored father, the celebrated criminal defense attorney Earl Rogers, and their host, the famous writer Jack London.

Then came the memorable afternoon when Jack and Earl left for an afternoon visit to a neighbor. "For five days," Adela recalled, "nobody heard a word," until, suddenly, the two men appeared side by side astride burros and belting a waterfront ballad, "Whiskey, Johnny, Whiskey":

> WHISKEY-O, JOHNNY-O
> John rise her up from down below
> Whiskey, whiskey, whiskey-o
> Up aloft this yard must go
> John rise her up from down below
> Whiskey-o, Johnny-o

"I could not understand what I was seeing," a bewildered Adela recalled, although many years later, when she had become Adela Rogers St. Johns, the prominent journalist, the scene unfolded with crystal clarity: the father who successfully defended clients who were charged with the most heinous crimes could not defend himself against the ravages of alcohol, which cut short Earl Rogers's career and sent him to an early grave. The world-famous Jack London ultimately succumbed as well, but only after penning some fifty books, including *John Barleycorn*, which the tough-minded Adela Rogers St. Johns declared to be "an autobiographical masterpiece . . . the best book ever written on alcohol."

Titled after a popular nickname for liquor, a derivation of the distilled grains barley and corn, the book both embodied and personified the power of John Barleycorn. Jack London claimed him as a character, an alter ego who would take center stage in the memoir, but only after readers had weathered accounts of London's youthful take-it-or-leave-it flirtations with beer, wine, and whiskey in his multiple lives as a California farm boy, sailor, college student, laborer, Klondike gold hunter, yachtsman, ranchman, writer—and. finally, public intellectual and bon vivant.

John Barleycorn slowly seduced Jack London before it took him captive completely in his later thirties. His "preliminary cocktail" at dinner parties engendered a "kindly, genial glow," and social drinking became "an act of comradeship and accepted hospitality." Though occasionally, London admitted, he felt "well jingled," a cocktail sometimes fueled his literary energies and ferried him through oh-so-many evenings in the company of dullards. ("A cocktail or two, before dinner, enabled me to laugh whole-heartedly. . . . The cocktail was a prod, a spur, a kick to my jaded mind and bored spirits.")

In time, London surrendered to John Barleycorn when he craved cocktails, morning to night—and drank alone. "I was never interested enough in cocktails to know how they were made," he wrote. "So I got a bar-keeper in Oakland to make them in bulk and ship them to me." The barkeeper may well have been the mixologist at Oakland's Saddle Rock Café, an elegant restaurant where London and his wife often dined, and the writer relished pressed duck, washed down with liebfraumilch, a German white wine. As for the cocktails, we must speculate, though a bartender mixing for Jack had two clues: the famous writer's love of candy and his background as a sailor, including his travels to Cuba, the home of Bacardi rum. A sweet rum cocktail would fit the bill.

Any bartender looking to mix cocktails in quantity might have referred to the pocket-sized guide *Drinks as They Are Mixed: A Manual of Quick Reference* (1904), which included a chapter on "Recipes for Making Drinks in Bulk for Bottling."

COCKTAIL (WHISKEY)

Ingredients

> 5 gallons bourbon or rye whiskey
>
> 2 gallons water
>
> I quart gum syrup
>
> 2 ounces tincture of orange peel
>
> I ounce gentian
>
> ½ ounce cardamom

Directions

> 1. Mix all ingredients together.
> 2. Color with equal parts caramel and solferino.

"CURE"

Evalyn Walsh (b. 1886) began life in Colorado log cabins and slumbered in flannel Union suits, never dreaming that she would one day own the Hope Diamond and order evening gowns from the House of Worth, the preeminent Parisian courtier. Her storied rags-to-riches tale began when her Irish immigrant father, Thomas F. Walsh, whispered to ten-year-old Evalyn, "Daughter, I've struck it rich."

Walsh's declaration upended family life for her parents and for Evalyn and her younger brother, Vincent. The vein of gold that Thomas Walsh discovered in the Colorado Rocky Mountains made the family superlatively wealthy and boosted them to heights of social and political influence. The Walshes traveled in their own private railroad car and in first-class suites for ocean crossings, if not aboard a friend's yacht. Their summer leisure included weeks at Newport, Rhode Island, and Bar Harbor, Maine, the resorts of the wealthy and powerful. Evalyn was seventeen years of age when her parents hosted a ball in honor of Miss Alice Roosevelt, the president's daughter, in the Louis XIV–styled salon of the Walsh family mansion in Washington, DC.

Though Evalyn declared that "It Is No Fun to Be a Lady" (a chapter in her memoir), she maximized her new-found celebrity and wealth. European princes came courting, but she shooed them off to marry her childhood sweetheart, Ned (Edward Beale McLean), a wealthy Washington, DC, newspaper heir (of both the *Washington Post* and *Cincinnati Enquirer*). As newlyweds, Evalyn and Ned honeymooned in Mercedes motorcars in "Dresden, Leipzig, Cologne, Dusseldorf," each featuring a memorable "shopping spree"—after which the couple traveled to St. Petersburg and Constantinople (now Istanbul), where Evalyn met the sultan, ruler of the Ottoman Empire. The couple would soon settle in the nation's capital and become the parents of four children.

No one knew Evalyn's secret: her addiction to morphine.

The habit had gripped her from adolescence when, one Newport summer, an automobile accident proved fatal to her brother, Vincent, and left Evalyn severely injured and submerged in "waves of pain." She underwent experimental surgery to repair her badly crippled leg and chronicled the slow recovery and rehabilitation. "They gave me more and more morphine," she wrote, "and even then my pain would prowl." Years later, in 1910, when her beloved father died, Evalyn, who was now married and the mother of an infant, found that "grief over the loss of my father brought me back, temporarily, to morphine."

Though admitting that she was "more cunning than an animal in hiding her supply," Evalyn determined to kick the habit. Horrified at the prospect of an inpatient cure in asylum, she agreed to confine herself in a hotel suite under the watchful eye of her doctor, who "seated himself in a comfortable chair" to keep a nightlong vigil over a rebellious Evalyn. Declaring that she would open the throttle "on the road to hell," she defiantly called room service and ordered three Manhattan cocktails. "A hotel servant came and placed the tray of cocktails . . . on the mantelpiece," she recalled. All night long, she approached the cocktails, backed away, moved toward them, backed off once again, a push-pull that went on for hours, as the cocktails attracted and repelled—but distracted her from her craving for morphine. By dawn, the three Manhattans remained on the mantelpiece, untouched. "That was the last struggle I had with morphine," she declared.

Sadly, Ned McLean's own alcoholism eroded the marriage and hastened his business losses, but Evalyn also stressed the damage that unbridled wealth inflicted on their lives. "We had the money," she wrote, "or rather it had us. We were held fast in its clutches, held fast to it as I had been to morphine. Indeed, I think that is the way to say it: we were the slaves of an infernal habit. This habit stole our will, subtly metamorphosed our point of view, thwarted our creative powers, and quite constantly made us the victims of . . . greed."

MANHATTAN COCKTAIL

Ingredients

Half tumblerful of cracked ice

2 parts rye or bourbon whiskey

I part vino vermouth

2 dashes gum syrup

2 dashes bitters

I dash absinthe

Maraschino cherry (optional)

Directions

1. Combine ingredients in tumbler.

2. Stir well.

3. Strain and serve.

If desired, add Maraschino cherry.

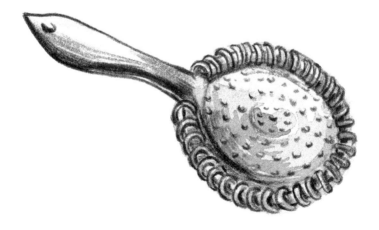

10

In Honor Of—

Gilded Age cocktails were often named for high-profile figures whose exploits, featured in the press, brought fame or notoriety worthy of street-corner conversation, parlor gossip—and the cocktail bar. Whether a war hero, an actress, a politician, a rascal or scamp, such individuals might inspire a daring mixologist to venture beyond his repertoire (and his reference manual) to leap into new territory and invent a beverage worthy of the annals of the Gilded Age.

BRADLEY MARTIN

An "accidental" millionaire, Bradley Martin (b. 1841) struck it rich when his wife, the former Cornelia Sherman, whom he'd met at the wedding of socialite Emily Vanderbilt, unexpectedly inherited a fortune from her deceased father, Isaac, a retired merchant in New York. Their new fortune radically altering the prospects for the couple's daughter, Cornelia, the Bradley-Martins (as they now styled themselves) would have sought advice in the how-to manual *Titled Americans: A List of American Ladies Who Have Married Foreigners of Rank* (1890). This veritable guide to husband hunting showed how "I do" at the altar could transform a daughter of wealthy American parents into a countess, a duchess, or perhaps even a princess.

The parental Martins' social ambitions vaulted toward the realms of royalty. Their strategic courtship on behalf of their daughter presumed a hefty dowry, for the titled husband-to-be typically suffered from severe financial anemia, to be remedied by one of America's "dollar princesses," an eligible young lady from the ranks of the nation's newly wealthy industrialists. In April 1894, sixteen-year-old Cornelia was married off to the twenty-five-year-old, heavily tattooed William George Robert, fourth Earl of Craven and Viscount of Uffington. Cornelia had become the Countess of Craven.

Newspapers covered the wedding in copious detail, but the bigger story was yet to come, for three years on, on the evening of February 10, 1897, the Bradley-Martins hosted Society for a costume ball at the Waldorf Hotel in one of the most spectacular social events of the Gilded Age. The interior of the hotel was transformed for the evening into a replica of Versailles and decorated with tapestries and roses. The eight hundred guests dressed as the historical royals with whom they most identified

(Mrs. Bradley-Martin attired as Mary, Queen of Scots, her husband as Louis XV). Though ostensibly billed by the Bradley-Martins as a philanthropic means to stimulate local spending in the midst of an economic depression, the extravagance and outlandish expense instantly fed the gossip mills and consumed newspaper columns for weeks. "If the Bradley-Martins were aware of unemployment, starvation . . . and widespread despair," the editorials chided, they showed no such sign.

The tally of cocktails at the ball is nowhere recorded, but Albert Stevens Crockett, a journalist and an observer of Gilded Age manners, did manage to obtain the inventory of the Bradley-Martins' beverage expenditures for the infamous ball. Savaging the era's strutting "peacocks on parade," he declared the drinks to have been a great bargain. "Only a little over nine thousand dollars for the . . . most lavish" party of its day, Crockett exclaimed.

Ballroom and Supper—700.................	$4,550.00
59-10/12 cases Moet & Chandon @ $50 a case....................................	2,991.70
4 bottles Irroy Brut @ $3.50.............	14.00
10 bottles Moet & Chandon WS @ $3.50..	35.00
55 bottles Château Mouton @ $2.25......	123.75
6 Medoc Superieur @ $.75...............	4.50
496 bottles Mineral Water @ $.30........	148.80
11 bottles Whiskey.....................	22.00
3 bottles Brandy......................	18.00
48 bottles Soda.......................	7.20
Beer and wine for musicians.............	43.50
Victor Herbert's band..................	658.00
Carl Berger's and Eden Musée bands......	250.00
Supper and cigars (probably including food for musicians and policemen)..........	150.00
Ribbons..............................	20.00
	$9,036.35

BRADLEY MARTIN COCKTAIL

Ingredients

1–2 ounces crème de menthe

Raspberry syrup

Ice

Directions

1. Pour crème de menthe over ice.

2. Add raspberry syrup as preferred and serve.

FLORADORA

American audiences welcomed the first "naughty" synchro-nized dance troupe when the Original Floradora Sextet took the stage in 1900 at New York's Casino Theatre, by way of London, wowing New York audiences for 552 per-formances. No longer need Americans cruise to Paris and the Folies Bergère or Moulin Rouge to feast eyes on scantily clad chorines. The Floradora girls had domestic forebears in an 1866 variety show production, *The Black Crook*, which created a "furor" when "ladies from foreign shores" min-gled with "American girls"—one hundred lassies appearing "in diaphanous robes" to "prance forth in a series of ballets which gave the chorus girl a place on the American stage." Her place secured by *The Black Crook*'s numerous revivals, the Floradora girls in their flesh-toned tights became the "toast of the town," according to the memoir *It Seems Like Yesterday* by playwright Russel Crouse (b. 1893). Legend had it, said Crouse, that "they all married millionaires they met at the stage door," and the cocktail in their honor toasted the girls, one and all.

THE FLORADORA

Ingredients

    1½ ounces gin

    Juice of 1 lime

    ½ teaspoon sugar

    ½ ounce raspberry syrup

    Ginger ale

Directions

1. Shake gin, lime juice, sugar, and syrup.
2. Pour into Collins glass with ice cubes.
3. Top with ginger ale and stir.

STEINWAY

Along with upholstered furniture, the piano became *de rigueur* in respectable American parlors from the later 1800s. Sheet music of popular tunes proliferated, and young ladies were expected to demonstrate a measure of competence at the eighty-eight black and white keys in evening musicales for friends and family. Piano music at its finest—by Brahms, Chopin, and, of course, Ludwig von Beethoven—resounded as well in the new Music Hall, established by Andrew Carnegie at the corner of 57th and Broadway in 1891, where the focal instrument onstage would no doubt have been a Steinway piano. The German immigrant Henry Steinway (born Heinrich Engelhard Steinweg), had opened his first piano factory in lower Manhattan in 1853 and by the 1860s the Steinway & Sons factory occupied a full city block on Park Avenue between Fifty-Second and Fifty-Third streets. His prize-winning pianos proved that high-quality instruments no longer needed to be imported from Europe, and Steinway pianos became the gold standard in concert halls, auditoriums, and American homes.

Among the "Sons" of Steinway, Charles H. (b. 1857), became a celebrated gourmand. Known as "Charles Steinway, the piano manufacturer" and a close friend of President Grover Cleveland, Steinway dined out often and lavishly. On one occasion he staged "a dinner that Lucullus would be proud of." According to Albert Stevens Crockett's Gilded Age memoir, *Peacocks on Parade* (1931), the dinner began with champagne cocktails (a blend of chilled champagne and amontillado sherry), followed by a formidable succession of courses partnered with rarest vintages consumed by the case. As a "matter of record," "Mr. Steinway and thirty-two guests, ladies as well as gentlemen, ate, in order: fancy deviled eggs, oysters, green turtle soup; a mousse of bass in the shape of a turban, with cucumbers; breast of chicken, with Madeira sauce; oyster crabs with mushrooms; saddle of lamb, braised with ham, together with potatoes and fresh peas; a sherbet, or water ice, flavored with rum or wine or brandy; terrapin in Philadelphia style; a canvasback duck, with current jelly; fancy ice cream and small cakes, followed by fruits and coffee."

"How men and women to the number of thirty-two could have got outside so much food and especially drink during a dinner must furnish a theme for wonder," concluded Crockett. "Speaking of appetites and capacity, there must have been giants—and giantesses—in those days." It is not known whether a pianist at a Steinway accompanied the feast with dinner music. If so, the model would undoubtedly have been a concert grand.

STEINWAY COCKTAIL

Ingredients

    1½ ounces whiskey (bourbon, rye, or scotch)

    ½ lemon

    ½ teaspoon sugar

    Fruit of choice

    Seltzer

Directions

    1. Muddle lemon in mixing glass.

    2. Add sugar and whiskey.

    3. Stir and strain into tall glass.

    4. Fill with chilled seltzer; decorate with fruit.

COMMODORE

In January 1877, commemorations for deceased railroad king-pin Cornelius Vanderbilt (b. 1794) hailed the departed tycoon as "the architect of his own fortune," a figure of "genius," and of "indomitable energy." One memorial stated, "The tru-est monument to Cornelius Vanderbilt is the fact that he so organized his creation that the work will go on, though the master workman is gone." Other tributes spooled from rail-road directors who owed their livelihoods to the patriarch of a transportation network that covered the US from the Atlantic seaboard to the Mississippi. This near-monopoly had been made possible, the directors averred, only because Vanderbilt was "essentially the creator . . . of the circumstances which he moulded to his purposes."

The Vanderbilt empire began with two small ferry boats plying the New York harbor from Staten Island to the docks of lower Manhattan. The ambitious teenage ferryman at the til-ler of a double-masted sailing craft in the early 1800s had his eye on the new steam engines and the possibilities for marine propulsion that would not depend on variable winds filling the sails. Rival ferrymen satirically nicknamed Cornelius the "Commodore," but, at the time, the notion of him becom-ing the commander of America's shipping and railroad lines would have been beyond farfetched.

The Vanderbilt story combines the invention of new tech-nology in the age of steam and steel, unfettered business en-terprise in a laissez-faire environment, and one individual's hellbent quest for autonomous, boundless power. The mile-stones included the leap to steam ferries in the New York–New Jersey waterways, to steamboats up the Hudson and other rivers, and thereafter to oceangoing shipping. At the age when a successful man might retire, Vanderbilt then turned to rail to amass his second great fortune. (His private rail car, *Vanderbilt*, was pulled by a locomotive likewise named *Vanderbilt*.) Along the way, shipping lanes and rail routes were strewn with court cases and vanquished rivals, but, by the 1860s, Vanderbilt "controlled American steamship traffic on the Atlantic Ocean," and the *Chicago Tribune* declared that Vanderbilt now had "almost kingly power."

T. J. Stiles's biography, *The First Tycoon*, triples Vanderbilt's lifetimes: "Captain," "Commodore," and "King." His sole great mark as a philanthropist was the one-million-dollar bequest for the founding of an institution of higher learning in Nashville, Tennessee: Vanderbilt University.

A figure of such magnitude, not surprisingly, earned two distinctly different versions of the cocktail mixed in his honor.

COMMODORE COCKTAIL #1

Ingredients

> 1½ ounces Bacardi rum
>
> 1 dash grenadine
>
> 1 dash raspberry syrup
>
> 1 dash lemon juice
>
> ½ teaspoon sugar
>
> 1 egg white

Directions

> 1. In shaker with ice, add rum.
>
> 2. Add all other ingredients.
>
> 3. Shake vigorously.
>
> 4. Strain and serve.

COMMODORE COCKTAIL #2

Ingredients

> 1 to 1½ ounces bourbon whiskey
>
> 1 to 1½ ounces crème de cacao
>
> 1 ounce lemon juice
>
> 1 dash grenadine

Directions

> 1. In mixing glass with ice, add whiskey, crème de cacao, and lemon juice.
> 2. Stir fully.
> 3. In champagne glass, add dash of grenadine.
> 4. Pour mixture into champagne glass and serve.

PEG O' MY HEART

In December 1912, the bright lights of Broadway blazed at the Cort Theatre on West Forty-Eighth Street for the opening of *Peg o' My Heart*, starring the winsome Laurette Taylor. The popular play inspired lyricist Alfred Bryan and tunesmith Fred Fisher to compose "Peg o' My Heart" the following year, which was sung and played from the late Gilded Age far into the twentieth century. The pre-karaoke era might have featured a few vocalists belting the tune, emboldened by the cocktail named for "Peg."

> Peg o' my heart,
> I'll love you
> Don't let us part
> I love you
> I always knew
> It would be you,
> Since I heard your lilting laughter

It's your Irish heart I'm after.
Peg o' my heart,
Your glances
Make my heart say,
How's chances?
Come be my own;
Come make your home in my heart.

PEG O' MY HEART COCKTAIL

Ingredients

1 to 1½ ounces Bacardi rum

½ to 1 ounce lime juice

Grenadine

Directions

1. In mixing glass with ice, add rum and lime juice.
2. Color with grenadine.
3. Stir, strain, and serve.

VAN WYCK

The year 1898 marked the consolidation of the five boroughs into one greater New York City. Manhattan ruled as the capital, but forged its urban identity with Brooklyn, Queens, Staten Island, and the only borough connected to the US mainland, the Bronx. "Gigantic, colossal, enormous, daring," one tourist described Gotham at the approach of the twentieth century. And 1898 was the year that Robert Anderson Van Wyck (b. 1849) took office as "His Honor, the Mayor." A Columbia University–trained attorney, he had spent years in Democratic party politics and served a stint as a municipal court judge. His name (pronounced "van wick") echoed the revered Old New Amsterdam of colonial days, but the new mayor had "no independent base, no money, no personal pizazz" and was thought to be a pawn of Tammany Hall's "Boss" Richard Croker. A scandal involving a monopolistic "ice trust" tainted his term, and Van Wyck was swept out of office in 1901. (The cocktail named for the mayor features ice.)

VAN WYCK COCKTAIL

Ingredients

> 1½ ounces Tom gin
>
> ½ ounce sloe gin
>
> 1 dash orange bitters

Directions

> 1. In mixing glass with ice, add Tom gin and sloe gin.
> 2. Add bitters.
> 3. Stir and strain into stemware glass.

HEARST

"A great man, able, self-dependent, and clear-headed" proclaimed a hard-nosed reporter in tribute to the controversial newspaper mogul William Randolph Hearst (b. 1863). Derided in many quarters for seducing a craven public with outlandish, fictionalized accounts of events, Hearst withstood critics and amassed a fortune—but not before he tapped family wealth to launch himself in the newspaper business in an era when the printed page was the social media of its day.

The son of a father who had reaped his own fortunes from Western mining, real estate, and cattle ranching (and served as a US senator), young "Bill" jolted the senior Hearst upon announcing his career ambition to enter newspaper publishing. Perhaps George Hearst hoped that his son would soon weary of journalism when he gifted him with the *San Francisco Examiner*, a paper in competition with others in the City by the Bay. The *Examiner* flourished under young Hearst's command, however, whetting his appetite for New York, for a newspaper publisher of cosmic ambition in the Gilded Age gauged success by helming a flagship paper in Gotham. Buying the *New York Journal* in 1895, Hearst went head-to-head against Joseph Pulitzer's *World* in the "newspaper wars" that also embroiled lesser combatants: the *Herald*, *Sun*, and *New York Times*. The two titans nearly bankrupted their papers in their coverage of the Spanish-American War of 1898. (A newsboys' strike helped prompt the titans' ceasefire.)

"Each of the great newspapers of New York," observed the visiting French journalist Paul Bourget, "is made in the image of him who edits it." While Hearst garnered a reputation for publishing factually false reportage known derisively as "yellow journalism," muckraking investigative reporter Lincoln Steffens profiled Hearst in 1906 as a "rich man" without "moral illusions" who sought "to give people democracy, as others of his sort give . . . an art museum." Hearst's machinery of democracy was described by Bourget, who marveled at modern newspaper production: a "formidable printing creature"—the printing press—"a multiplier of thought to an extent not measurable by any human arithmetic." The press roared, Bourget said, like Niagara, with its "gliding whiteness" to be "bent and folded by innumerable bars of steel" and "printed on both sides," a modern miracle of the industrial age.

HEARST COCKTAIL

Ingredients

1½ ounces Plymouth gin

1 ounce Italian vermouth

1 dash orange bitters

1 dash Angostura bitters

Directions

1. In mixing glass with ice, add gin and vermouth.

2. Add orange and Angostura bitters.

3. Stir, strain, and serve.

MAMIE GILROY

Stage actresses, with few exceptions, were suspected of impure lives offstage as "ladies of the night." Fortunately for Mamie Gilroy (b. 1871?), the ingénue was the niece of the mayor of New York City, Thomas Francis Gilroy. A democratic political party loyalist and acolyte of Tammany's "Boss" Tweed, Gilroy had climbed political stepping stones to a term in City Hall in 1893–94. He cast a cloak of respectability upon his niece—an especially important avuncular protection for an actress performing on the stages of conservative Boston and Philadelphia, as well as San Francisco and Seattle. Employed by the powerful Charles Frohman chain of theaters, which sent stock companies nationwide, Mamie performed steadily through the 1890s and opening years of the new century in such plays as *Romany Rye*, *The Merry-Go-Round*, and *The Girl from Paris*, in which she played the memorable Mademoiselle Julie Bon-Bon. The *Boston Globe* declared Mamie Gilroy "one of the brightest, most vivacious, and altogether most charming" of thespians.

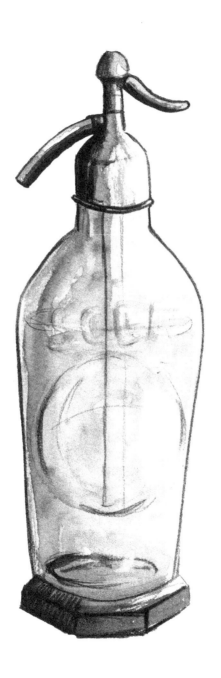

At times known as La Petite Gilroy, this "Girl from Paris" regrettably fell in love with a Chicago physician who, most inconveniently, had already tied the knot and kept a spouse in residence. Undaunted, in 1901 Mamie allowed the use of her name and picture to promote a "blood and nerve remedy" called Dr. Greene's Nervura, testifying in print that it had averted a nervous breakdown. Imbibers' nerves, on the other hand, might be soothed at the bar with a cocktail named in honor of the "most charming" of actresses.

MAMIE GILROY COCKTAIL

Ingredients

> 1½ ounces scotch whisky
>
> 1 dash Hostetter's bitters
>
> Juice of ½ lime
>
> 6–8 ounces chilled soda water

Directions

> 1. In Collins glass, squeeze lime.
> 2. Add whisky.
> 3. Add bitters.
> 4. Fill with soda and stir.

ARMOUR

"Daily employment to eleven thousand employees," exclaimed an awed European traveler, who marveled at the industrial strength of Chicago's modern meatpacking industry. The city formerly disparaged as "Porkopolis," he continued, had become a "great enterprise" of "colossal manufactures of roast beef and hams," and by 1895 Armour & Company was annually shipping 3.5 million "dressed cattle" to "the four parts of this immense continent." A tour of Armour's operation was admittedly nerve-wracking, he conceded, but a stunning exhibition of "American ingenuity."

As a youth, the Chicago stockyard "king" Philip Danforth Armour (b. 1832) left his family's farm in upstate New York to try his luck in the California gold rush of 1849, faring well enough to launch a wholesale grocery business in Cincinnati before relocating to Milwaukee. He profited handsomely from sales of meat to the Union Army in the Civil War, and, by 1875, Armour & Company had relocated to Chicago. Scaled for high volume and low cost, Armour's operation disassembled livestock with unprecedented speed and efficiency. With his major competitor, Augustus Swift, Armour's business threatened the livelihoods of thousands of small butchers who could not compete in price with the meat that was processed in Chicago and shipped hundreds or thousands of miles away, yet stayed fresh in refrigerated railroad cars and was sold at prices within reach of an expanding middle class.

Americans enjoying the newly affordable roast beef or pork chops had no idea that Mr. Armour broke even at best on the sale of the choice cuts of meat, which was far less profitable than the business in the bits that never made it to the table. From bone to fat, fur to hooves, a dizzying array of consumer products were manufactured from the packinghouse by-products. "I don't know," remarked the traveler, "who said that a pig that went to the abbatoir in Chicago came out fifteen minutes later in the form of ham, sausages . . . hair oil, and binding for a bible," but the "witty exaggeration is hardly overdone." It was not, for paint brushes, furniture upholstery, combs, and boot polish were but a few of the panoply of products that swelled Armour's coffers.

ARMOUR COCKTAIL

Ingredients

> I ounce sherry
> I ounce Italian vermouth
> 2 dashes orange bitters

Directions

> I. In mixing glass with ice, add sherry and vermouth.
> 2. Add orange bitters.
> 3. Stir, strain, and serve.

COXEY

The Ohio quarryman never served in the military nor rose to prominence as a "captain" of industry. Nevertheless, Jacob S. Coxey (b. 1854) was destined to lead a notable force in the annals of American social, political, and economic history. A rags-to-riches success, "Jake" Coxey rose from waterboy at an iron mill to the ownership of a Massillon, Ohio, quarry producing sand for glass and iron manufacture. By 1893, however, he became concerned about the plight of American workers, for mounting job losses had put thousands of men out of work, and the figures were worsening. A financial panic that year, precipitated by a run on gold, had shuttered five hundred banks and driven major railroads into bankruptcy. Over fifteen thousand companies failed, and up to 18 percent of the workforce was unemployed. How would families eat when work itself had vanished?

Like many of his generation, Coxey remembered the wrenching seven years' depression of the 1870s, and he knew the current massive layoffs were not workers' fault. Though no unemployment insurance program existed, Congress had authorized pensions for wounded veterans of the Union and Confederate armies, and also for deceased veterans' widows and orphaned young children. Surely the congressmen, if they came face to face with the jobless workers, would recognize their plight as a similar crisis and act to provide jobs and a measure of relief.

In 1894, Coxey mustered four hundred men to march the four hundred miles from Massillon to Washington, DC, a "petition in boots" on behalf of the right to work for a living. The ragtag band, dubbed "Coxey's Army" by the press, were no armed militia, but an assemblage of the jobless. Similar "armies" set forth from the Pacific Northwest and Southern California, but Congress, for its part, was unmoved when the men reached the nation's capital. Jacob Coxey was arrested for walking on the grass of the US Capitol.

COXEY COCKTAIL

Ingredients

> 1½ ounces Plymouth gin
>
> 1½ ounces Italian vermouth
>
> 1 dash Amer Picon bitters

Directions

> 1. In mixing glass with ice, add gin and vermouth.
> 2. Add bitters.
> 3. Stir, strain, and serve.

SAM WARD

"The business of lobbying is as precarious as fishing in the Hebrides," lamented politician Samuel Cutler Ward (b. 1814). "You get all ready, your boats go out—suddenly there comes a storm, and away you are driven." The legendary King of the Lobby, Ward did not casually compare fishing the corridors of political power to the North Sea blasts. If the word "lobbyist" lacked cachet, it was literally grounded, named for the paved halls outside legislators' offices and chambers where favor seekers and petitioners waiting to plead their causes and cases when the lawmakers exited their sanctums. Decades of experience in the nation's capital taught him that the odds of success in a legislative session were slim. The "sure thing" could melt away like a late spring snowfall.

Sam (as he was called) was, until midlife, something of a dilettante. The son of a New York banker (and one of seven children), he grieved his mother's tragic death during his school days and found banking too distasteful to follow in his father's footsteps. He compiled a middling record at Columbia College, and extensive European travels failed to sharpen his career focus, though they refined his epicurean palette. A mercantile venture in San Francisco during the gold rush days ended in a warehouse fire and serious financial losses, and his first marriage, in 1838, to John Jacob Astor's granddaughter Emily Astor, had ended tragically after only three years when she and the infant died at the child's birth. It was only in 1859, as the Civil War loomed, that Sam Ward, at forty-four years of age, arrived in Washington at a most auspicious time.

The expansive reach of the federal government after the Civil War ripened opportunities—and possibly the necessity—for lobbyists. From financial policy to pensions, agriculture to education, the US government now reached deeply into Americans' lives. The prolific Gilded Age chronicler James Dabney McCabe's *Behind the Scenes in Washington* (1873), written under the pseudonym Edwin Winslow Martin, dubbed Washington "the centre from which radiate the varied influences which affect every citizen of the Republic from the millionaire to the man dependent on his daily earnings." Savvy insiders knew they must find favor, not only with Congress and the White House, but within the various bureaus and commissions ballooning in the nation's capital. In 1861, some 2,199 civilian employees of the federal government worked in the capital; by 1881, the number had risen to 14,124. The times demanded navigators who could plot the way through the labyrinth, all the while aware of the final destination: a law favorable for the client.

The King of the Lobby succeeded on the strength of his "gift for friendship," an ability to cultivate cordial relationships with people of radically different political convictions who found the roundabout manner of doing business during "ambrosial evenings" at his dining table more pleasant and efficacious than haggling in drafty congressional corridors, offices, or conference rooms. At his most influential, Ward numbered the nation's manufacturers, steamship lines, mining interests, banks, railroads, and insurance companies among his clients. Though the Crédit Mobilier scandal, which broke in 1872, ensnared dozens of politicians in a scheme by the Union Pacific Railroad to inflate construction costs, pocket millions, and bribe politicians for favorable regulation—Sam Ward remained untouched. "We keep up a certain circle of friends," he said, "and once in a while a certain opportunity comes of getting something that is of real service, and for which compensation is due and proper." The Sam Ward cocktail was his own invention.

SAM WARD COCKTAIL

Ingredients

Yellow Chartreuse

Lemon peel

Finely chipped ice

Directions

1. Fill tall glass with ice.
2. Rub lemon peel around rim of glass.
3. Fill with yellow Chartreuse.

11

The Bitter(s) Truth

By the dash, Gilded Age cocktails called for Angostura, orange, Peychaud's, or other bitters. The Sazerac demanded Peychaud's, the Old Fashioned its Angostura, the Mamie Gilroy a dash of Hostetter's, and so on. A bartender dared not serve a drink minus the crucial dash or two of the mysterious accent. Before bitters earned its stripes at the cocktail bar, however, it was first liberated from clinical service.

Bitters entered the bar by way of the apothecary, for extracts of botanicals were long thought to promote health. A "Treatise" of 1897, intended for druggists (and, surprisingly, confectioners too) defined "BITTERS": "These are made by extracting bitter and aromatic—or bitter only—drugs with a mixture of alcohol and water; sometimes a small amount of sugar or syrup is added." These botanical "drugs" included herbs, spices, flowers, citrus peels, and, for the best-known bitters, the bark of the Angostura tree. All were extracted and compounded into tonics thought to be curative for digestive woes, stomach troubles, even gout. Sufferers often believed that the bitterer the dose, the more effective, and so extremely bitter botanicals were favored such as ground pine, wormwood leaves, and elfdock root, most of their efficacy a credit to the placebo effect. Alcohol was the main solvent used to tease the flavors and essential oils from the botanicals (comparable to brewing tea). The process proceeds to filtration, and to the heating and cooling of distillation. By volume, the finished, bottled bitters ranked—and rank today—high in alcoholic content. Among the most familiar, Angostura is 44.7 percent and orange is often 45 percent.

The apothecary's mortar and pestle did not immediately segue to the bartender's muddler, but pharmacies had long sold wines, and alcohol was a mainstay of numerous tonics. Experimentation was inevitable, and one bitters, Peychaud's, is historically notable as a case in point. During the slaves' revolt on the Caribbean island of Saint-Domingue in the 1790s, the wealthy Peychaud family pondered flight to New Orleans. They escaped from the island a short time later, in 1803, just a year before it became the independent nation of Haiti. In New Orleans, Antoine (b. 1803) grew up to become a pharmacist who experimented with bitters produced from the Caribbean spices of his heritage, most probably as a medicinal tonic. A few drops added to cognac pleased his customers, and Peychaud is credited with compounding the first commercially successful bitters, which is said to have "a bitingly sharp and medicinal orangish-cherry flavor."

The bitters battles include long-gone brands, such as Hostetter's Stomach Bitters, Flint's Quaker Bitters, Mandrake Bitters, Atwood's Jaundice Bitters, and Drake's Plantation Bitters. Connoisseurs of bitters exult in their recent revival, but ordinary imbibers know one name only: Angostura.

ACKNOWLEDGMENTS

This book bubbled to life over predinner springtime cocktails in Tarrytown, New York, as literary agent Deirdre Mullane and I mused about cocktails of the Gilded Age. Deirdre had worked closely with me on *What Would Mrs. Astor Do? The Essential Guide to the Manners and Mores of the Gilded Age*. That romp through New York's glittering era of Fifth Avenue mansions and Wall Street ticker tapes had taken notice of the champagnes and rare wines of the time, but perhaps had slighted its most "spirited" beverages.

As Deirdre and I sipped and savored ("too sweet? too bitter? salty?"), we decided the moment was ripe for this project. The present era of the "Lives of the *Superrich* and Famous"—and devotion to craft cocktails—might launch a time-traveler's journey to the beverages of the first Gilded Age. The ingenious "founders" who tended ancestral American bars surely left a mixological legacy that undergirds the current cocktail renaissance. The drinks they served, and named, would tell us much about their time—and shed light on our own.

Toasting the plan, we once again sought the favor of Clara Platter, senior editor at New York University Press, who had signed and overseen the publication of the elegant, sumptuous *What Would Mrs. Astor Do?* Without hesitation, Clara and her colleagues committed the press to produce *Gilded Age Cocktails*. A book is a team effort, and my gratitude goes to the editorial, design, production, advertising, and marketing professionals at NYU Press! And I send special thanks to the artist Julia Mills for her many illustrations that evoke the Gilded Age and its cocktail culture.

Friends and colleagues at Vanderbilt University toasted this project, for which I say "Thank you!" Special thanks to New Orleans native Thadious Davis, who lent helpful books, and to Evana Ahsan for keyboard speed and good cheer. I "pop" a cork for Valerie Hotchkiss, the dean of libraries at Vanderbilt University, who linked me to troves of Gilded Age archival documents and arranged the purchase of the rare edition of *The Old Waldorf-Astoria Bar Book*, my *vade mecum* for this project. Valerie's help and advice to "Have fun" is the model of an author's best send-off.

A book launches from the shoulders of its predecessors. *Gilded Age Cocktails* wraps each drink in the culture that produced it, but the professors of mixology enrolled this author in their required course in the alchemy of alcohols. Much is owed to Wayne Curtis, Adam Elmegirab, Iain Gately, William Grimes, Mark Lander, Brad Thomas Parsons, Charles Schumann, and David Wondrich, each of whose books is foundational and a "must" for anyone interested in beverages of the brewery, the wine cask, the distillery.

GLOSSARY

From The Old Waldorf-Astoria Bar Book

ABSINTHE—Usually a green, bitter, aromatic liquor, impregnated with wormwood, though there was also a white variety manufactured in France. *Deriv.*, Latin, *absinthium*, "wormwood." Long a resort for parodists in such lines as "Absinthe makes the heart grow fonder." Taken "neat" and often, was guaranteed to produce visions of snakes, etc.

ANISETTE—A liquor made in France by distillation from anise seed.

APPLEJACK—Often used synonymously with apple brandy or apple whiskey and supposed to be a distillation. New Jersey continued producing the one—or the three—right through prohibition.

AROMATIC SPIRITS OF AMMONIA—A fragrant distillation from a colorless, pungent, suffocating gas (NH3) obtained from nitrogenous organic bodies, such as coal, bones, blood, etc.

BENEDICTINE—A cordial or liqueur, distilled for centuries at Fécamp, in France, by the Benedictine monks. Its composition was kept secret and some persons believed its distillation was accompanied by religious rites. However, after the French revolution, discovery was made that it could be produced by the laity and by strictly secular methods. Its components have been kept a trade secret of cardamom seeds, arnica flowers, angelica root, lemon peel, thyme, nutmegs, cassia, hyssop, peppermint, and cloves. Imitation of Benedictine is not so much confined to prohibition history as patrons of bootleggers may have become convinced. As a matter of fact, such has been going on in France and elsewhere for generations, the average customer who did not know being satisfied if the bottle was queer and squat and bore the initials "D.O.M."

BITTERS—Beverages containing alcohol, together with a component for cathartic effect. Best known varieties: Angostura, made from the bark of a South American tree; Calisaya, synonymous with cinchona or quinine, also of South American origin; Orange; Boonekamp, made in Germany; Boker's, Amer Picon (which a stenographer rendered for me "American Pecan," but which is really a French proprietary proposition); Hostetter's, West Indies, Pepsin, Peychaud (formerly made in New Orleans); Fernet Branca, etc. So named from the usual bitter taste.

BRANDY—(Sometimes called "cognac," from a town in France noted for its manufacture.) Alcoholic liquor distilled from wine. *Deriv.*, Dutch, *brandewijn*, meaning "burnt wine." Was also made from the juice of apricots, peaches, apples or other fruit by distillation, and called liqueur. Cognac was often called for by the name of its maker, though in other days it was often referred to by the symbol printed on its label, "★★★" or "★★★★★," as indulgers frequently proved unable to read when ready for an encore.

CHARTREUSE—A distillation with brandy of certain rare herbs, used as a cordial or liqueur. The name was derived from the fact that Chartreuse, like Benedictine, owed its invention to early French monks, who knew about what they wanted and got it. These monks were of the Carthusian Order, and the liqueur was made only at their monastery in the Grande Chartreuse, in the French Alps. The formula for its preparation was said to be known only to the Father Superior of the Order. When the monks were expelled from France, in 1903, they spirted the secret of its preparation to Tarragona, in Spain, whence comes an herb much esteemed by gourmets in the treatment of vinegar. Rival manufactories were then set up in France, but their product was never so good as the original brand. Some thirty years or so before their expulsion, the Carthusian monks had suffered a big loss in the destruction of their brandy warehouse, wherein was stored what was said to be the largest stock of old Napoleon brandy in existence. Even before probation came, as much as twenty dollars a bottle was paid in New York for Chartreuse dated 1869 or before. While the monks have kept their formula a secret, analysts have named among the ingredients of Chartreuse: balm leaves, orange peel, dried hyssop tops, peppermint, wormwood, angelica seed and root, cinnamon, mace, cloves, Tonka beans, *calamus aromaticus* and cardamom. Some of the flavor, if not virtues of the product, however, was ascribed to certain herbs which were said to grow only in the neighborhood of the Grande Chartreuse. There were three varieties of Chartreuse—yellow, green, and white.

COINTREAU—A liqueur made in France, but not well known in the United States before prohibition.

CRÈME DE CACAO—An extract of cocoa, made in France. Used as a cordial or liqueur.

CRÈME DE CASSIS—A liqueur made in France of black currants, whose voltage still causes headaches to some who recall its potency.

CRÈME DE MENTHE—A distillation of mint, or of brandy flavored with mint. Usually green in color, though there is also a white variety. By those who could not pronounce its name correctly, it was often called "green mint," or "white mint," *menthe* being the French word for "mint." It is usually made in France.

CRÈME YVETTE—An extract of violets, used for flavoring purposes; also drunk as a cordial or liqueur. Its perfume often gave it preference over the common or garden refuge of the drinking dissembler—a clove or peppermint lozenge—before the commercial discovery of halitosis. Made in New York.

CURAÇAO—Often mispronounced "Curacoa," especially by Englishmen. A liquor made by distilling spirits with orange peel and certain spices. Manufactured originally in Holland. Name derived from that of a Dutch island off the north coast of South America.

DUBONNET—A proprietary French bitters or tonic, one of whose ingredients is said to be quinine.

GIN—Originally a drink distilled from malt or other grain and afterwards rectified with and flavored with juniper berries. Manufactured in Holland, under the name of Hollands, Schiedam, and Schnapps. For the effect of Schnapps, see Washington Irving's tale of that sterling New Yorker of pre-war times, *Rip Van Winkle*. Also manufactured in England under various names, notably: Gordon, Booth's, Holloway's, Old Tom, Nicholson, Plymouth, House of Lords, etc. Among the lower classes of London, "gin" is alcohol, flavored with oil of turpentine and common salt. The term is often used generically for "bad liquor." In some parts of the Cotton Belt, "gin" signifies a beverage whose effects are momentarily synonymous with those produced by the saws of a cotton gin—from which it is *not* derived. The actual derivation is from the Dutch *jenever*, itself coming from the old French word *jenevre*, meaning juniper. Gin was sometimes called "Geneva," "Geneva Water," and ascribed to Swiss invention.

SLOE GIN—Not to be confused with the real gin, and it should be noted that as compared with real gin, its effects are described by its first name, differently spelled. Sloe Gin is a sort of cordial made by distillation from the small, plumlike astringent fruit of the Blackthorn, or a distillation flavored with the same.

GRAND MARNIER—A cordial, or liqueur, made in France from oranges.

GRENADINE—A red syrup or cordial, said to be made from pomegranates; manufactured in France.

KIRSCH or KIRSCHWASSER—A liquor distilled from European wild cherries, and made in Germany and other central European countries.

KÜMMEL or KIMMEL—A liquor made generally from highly rectified alcohol, flavored with cumin (a plant of the parsley family) and caraway seed. Before the War it was manufactured chiefly at Riga, then in Russia.

MARASCHINO (pronounced "maraskeeno")—A cordial distilled from fermented cherries and flavored with bruised pits. *Deriv.*, Italian, *marasquino*

OJEN—A cordial formerly made in New Orleans, La., and flavored with absinthe.

ORGEAT—A syrup made in France from sugar, orange flower water and almonds. *Deriv.*, French, from Latin, *hordeum*, barley.

PARFAIT D'AMOUR—A red cordial whose composition was a proprietary secret, but whose name often assured those who had a slight acquaintance with French that it was a sort of love potion.

RUM—Generally, the name of any alcoholic liquor. Used as an adjective, colloquial English for "queer" or "peculiar." Specifically, an alcoholic liquor distilled from fermented molasses, or cane juice. Varieties usually named from country of origin—Jamaica, Swedish, St. Croix (West Indies), Cuban—better known as Bacardi or Santiago—and Japanese (usually called Sake and distilled from fermented rice). *Deriv.*, abbreviation of "rumbullion" or "rumbooze." The latter term is composed of the gypsy word *rom* or *rum*, meaning "good," and "booze," a corruption of the Dutch *bouse*, meaning to "guzzle," but now used as a good English word with a sinister meaning. The manufacture of rum was at one time an important New England industry, antedating that of cotton cloth. See "Jamaican Jollifiers."

SHERRY—Originally meant the white wine of Jerez, Spain, from whose name it was derived. Jerez was pronounced "Hareth," or "Herreth." The English corruption may have been due to excessive sibilance manifested by the original Britisher who drank a bottle and demanded more.

SODA, SIPHON, PLAIN SODA, CARBONIC, SELTZER, VICHY—Water charged with gas and discharged into a glass by pressing a lever controlling the metal vent of a siphon. CLUB SODA, aerated water in a small bottle. LEMON SODA, the same with a flavor of synthetic lemon. DELATOUR SODA, a brand of a particular manufacturer. The word VICHY was a misnomer, appropriated from that of the famous water bottled at Vichy, France, by the French Government.

SWEDISH PUNSCH—A beverage manufactured in Sweden, and having somewhat of the taste and properties of Rum.

VERMOUTH—A liquor made from white wine, flavored with aromatic herbs. Formerly, of the two varieties, the Italian, or sweet, was made in Italy, and the French, or *sec* (dry), was manufactured in France. A *sec* Vermouth is also made in Italy. *Deriv.*, German, *wermuth*, meaning "wormwood." In the country of its origin, Vermouth is often drunk "neat," that is to say unmixed with water or more potent liquids.

VIN MARIANI—A wine made in France from cocoa, and formerly very much advertised as a tonic.

WHISKEY—Again less comprehensive in definition than of late years, whiskey is an alcoholic liquor obtained by the distillation of a fermented starchy compound, usually a grain. *Deriv.*, Gaelic, *uisgebeatha*, "water of life." It used to be called also *eau de vie* or *aqua vitae*, meaning the same as the Gaelic term. The Swedes appropriated the name for "Aquavit," now one of their national drinks. Varieties: rye whiskey, made from that product; corn whiskey, called "Bourbon" if manufactured in Kentucky, and blended with rye, but turned out as "White Mule," "Moonshine" and under other names in illicit distilleries through the South; "Scotch," named for the country of its origin and popularly supposed to be made of oatmeal, the national dish, turned into spirits by the aid of peat fires, but more probably of barley or other grain, and "Irish," made in Ireland.

WINE—The juice of grapes, fermented by nature, in course of time. Varieties named in the compendium include Claret, the ordinary red wine of certain districts in France; Burgundy, the heavy red wine of Bourgogne, France; Madeira, the wine of the Portuguese Island of that name; Port, a wine whose name came from the Portuguese city of Oporto, whence it was exported; Rhine, meaning a wine made of grapes grown in the Rhine valley; Beaunne, wines both red and white, made in the vicinity of Beaune, France, and about the same voltage as Burgundy; Bordeaux, made grapes grown in the territory contiguous to the city of Bordeaux, France; Champagne, an effervescent wine made before the war in the Marne region of France, particularly at Rheims.

BAR GLASSES

Among the glasses mentioned as proper for the service of the fancy potations, the name "star" appears frequently. According to surviving authorities on bar-containers of the period, a "star" was synonymous with a SOUR glass.

The sour glass, so called because it was used for "sours" of various kinds, held from five and a half to six ounces. The LEMONADE was originally a thick goblet, but in time it became a thin, straight-sides glass, holding from six to eight ounces. The latter was originally the same as FIZZ or a HIGH-BALL glass. The COLLINS started out by being an eight-ounce glass, but a demand for a longer drink let to the adoption of a twelve- or even a sixteen-ounce glass—one that, besides the gin and the ice, would hold a "split" of soda. The CHAMPAGNE was usually a wide-bowled, thin-stemmed goblet; often, however, a thin four-ounce tumbler was also used, the same being also called an APOLLINARIS glass. A SHERRY glass was a small glass with a sharp, conical bowl, holding from three-quarters of an ounce to about an ounce and a third. A PONY was identical with a small liqueur glass, and held a scant ounce. A POUSE CAFÉ glass was an elongated pony, holding about an ounce and a half. A WHISKEY was a thin, low, straight-sided vessel holding about four ounces. The CLARET, a thin goblet, held from three and a half to four ounces.

The JIGGER was a conical metal container, holding about two ounces. In many establishments its use was abandoned in favor of the barman's eye. He was supposed to be able to gauge a jiggerful when pouring from a bottle in composing mixed drinks. In first class establishments, the customer was usually permitted to measure his own whiskey when he took it "neat," or in a high-ball.

BIBLIOGRAPHY

Adams, Ramon F. *Western Words: A Dictionary of the Range, Cow Camp, and Trail*. Norman: University of Oklahoma Press, 1944.

Allmendinger, David F. *Paupers and Scholars: The Transformation of Student Life in Nineteenth-Century New England*. New York: St. Martin's, 1975.

Asbury, Herbert. *The Barbary Coast: An Informal History of the San Francisco Underworld*. 1933. Reprint. New York: Thunder's Mouth Press, 2002.

———. Introduction to *The Bon-Vivant's Companion, or, How to Mix Drinks*, by Jerry Thomas, vi–xlvi. New York: Alfred A. Knopf, 1929.

Baldwin, Charles W. *Geography of the Hawaiian Islands*. New York: American Book Company, 1908.

Barr, Luke. *Ritz & Escoffier: The Hotelier, the Chef, & the Rise of the Leisure Class*. New York: Clarkson Potter, 2018.

Batterberry, Michael and Ariane. *On the Town in New York from 1776 to the Present*. New York: Charles Scribner's Sons, 1973.

Bourget, Paul. *Outre-Mer: Impressions of America*. New York: Charles Scribner's Sons, 1895.

Bramson, Seth H. *The Greatest Railroad Story Ever Told: Henry Flagler & the Florida East Coast Railway's Key West Extension*. Charleston, SC: History Press, 2011.

Brennan, Ella, and Dick Brennan. *The Commander's Palace New Orleans Cookbook*. New York: Clarkson Potter, 1984.

Burrows, Edwin G., and Mike Wallace, eds. *Gotham: A History of New York City to 1898*. New York: Oxford University Press, 1999.

Cather, Willa. *A Lost Lady*. New York: Alfred A. Knopf, 1939.

Clark, Susie. *The Round Trip from the Hub to the Golden Gate*. 1890. Reprint. Carlisle, MA: Applewood Books, n.d.

Crockett, Albert S. *The Old Waldorf-Astoria Bar Book*. New York: Dodd, Mead and Company, 1934.

———. *Peacocks on Parade: A Narrative of a Unique Period in American Social History and Its Most Colorful Figures*. New York: Sears, 1931.

Crouse, Russel. *It Seems Like Yesterday*. Garden City, New York: Doubleday, Doran, & Company, 1931.

Crowninshield, Francis. *Manners for the Metropolis: An Entrance Key to the Fantastic Life of the 400*. New York: D. Appleton, 1909.

Curtis, Wayne. *And a Bottle of Rum: A History of the New World in Ten Cocktails*. New York: Broadway, 2006.

Day, Clarence, Jr. *The Best of Clarence Day*. New York: Alfred A. Knopf, 1948.

De Courcy, Anne. *The Husband Hunters: American Heiresses Who Married the British Aristocracy*. New York: St. Martin's, 2017.

Dunlop, M. H. *Gilded City: Scandal and Sensation in Turn-of-the-Century New York*. New York: William Morrow, 2000.

Elmegirab, Adam. *Dr. Adam Elmigirab's Book of Bitters*. London: Dog 'n' Bone Books, 2017.

Erenberg, Lewis A. *Steppin' Out: New York Nightlife and the Transformation of American Culture, 1890–1930*. 1981. Reprint. Chicago: University of Chicago Press, 1984.

Escoffier, Auguste. *The Escoffier Cook Book: A Guide to the Fine Art of Cookery*. 1903. Reprint. New York: Crown, 1941.

Forbes, Cochran. *The Journals of Cochran Forbes: Missionary to Hawaii, 1831–1864*. Honolulu: Hawaiian Mission Children's Society, 1984.

Gately, Iain. *Drink: A Cultural History of Alcohol*. New York: Gotham, 2008.

Glazier, Willard. *Peculiarities of American Cities*. Philadelphia: Hubbard Brothers, 1885.

Grover, Janice Zita. "Luxury and Leisure in Early Nineteenth-Century America: Saratoga Springs and the Rise of the Resort." PhD diss., University of California, Davis, 1973.

Harris, Neil. *Humbug: The Art of P. T. Barnum*. Chicago: University of Chicago Press, 1973.

Holmes, Timothy. *Saratoga Springs: A Brief History*. Charleston, SC: History Press, 2008.

Holmes, Timothy, and Martha Stonequist. *Saratoga Springs: A Historical Portrait*. Charleston, SC: Arcadia Publishing, 2000.

Jackson, Kenneth J., ed. *The Encyclopedia of New York City*. New York: Yale University Press/Historical Society of New York City, 1995.

Jacob, Kathryn Allamong. *King of the Lobby: The Life and Times of Sam Ward, Man-about-Washington in the Gilded Age*. Baltimore: Johns Hopkins University Press, 2010.

James, Henry. *The American Scene*. 1907. Reprint. Bloomington: Indiana University Press, 1968.

Johnson, Harry. *Harry Johnson's New and Improved Bartender's Manual*. 1882. Reprint. Eastford, CT: Martino Fine Books, 2015.

Johnson, Owen. *Stover at Yale*. 1911. Reprint. Washington, DC: Ross & Perry, 2002.

Joki, Robert. *Saratoga Lost*. Delmar, NY: Black Dome Press, 1998.

Kaplan, Justin. *When the Astors Owned New York: Blue Bloods and Grand Hotels in a Gilded Age*. New York: Plume, 2007.

Lander, Mark Edward, and James Kirby Martin. *Drinking in America: A History*. New York: Free Press, 1987.

Logan, Andy. *The Man Who Robbed the Robber Barons*. 1965. Reprint. New York: Akadine Press, 2001.

London, Jack. *John Barleycorn*. 1913. Reprint. Orinda, CA: Sea Wolf Press, 2017.

Longworth, Alice Roosevelt. *Crowded Hours*. 1933. Reprint. New York: Arno, 1980.

Lowe, Corinne. *Confessions of a Social Secretary*. 1917. Reprint. Memphis, TN: General Books, 2012.

Lowe, Paul, ed. *Drinks as They Are Mixed: A Manual of Quick Reference*. Chicago: Frederick J. Drake, 1904.

Morris, Edmund. *The Rise of Theodore Roosevelt*. 1979. Reprint. New York: Library of America, 2001.

Murdock, Catherine Gilbert. *Domesticating Drink: Women, Men, and Alcohol in America, 1870–1940*. Baltimore: Johns Hopkins University Press, 1998.

Okrent, Daniel. *Last Call: The Rise and Fall of Prohibition*. 2010. Reprint. New York: Scribner, 2011.

Parsons, Brad Thomas. *Bitters: A Spirited History of a Classic Cure-All*. Berkeley, CA: Ten Speed Press, 2011.

Pulitzer, Ralph. *New York Society on Parade*. 1910. Reprint. London: FB&c Ltd, 2015.

Roberts, Charles G. D. *The Canadian Guide-Book*. New York: D. Appleton and Company, 1899.

Rydell, Robert W., John E. Findling, and Kimberly D. Pelle. *Fair America: World's Fairs in the United States*. Washington, DC: Smithsonian Institution Press, 2000.

Sala, George Augustus. *America Revisited: From the Bay of New York to the Gulf of Mexico*. London: Vizatelly & Co., 1882.

Schmidt, A. William. *The Flowing Bowl: When and What to Drink*. 1892. Reprint. Bedford, MA: Applewood Books, 2008.

Schumann, Charles. *American Bar: The Artistry of Mixing Drinks*. New York: Abbeville, 1995.

Sherwood, M. E. W. *The Art of Entertaining*. New York: Dodd, Mead, 1892.

Sinclair, Upton. *The Autobiography of Upton Sinclair*. New York: Harcourt, Brace & World, 1962.

Sklar, Kathryn Kish. *Florence Kelley and the Nation's Work*. New Haven, CT: Yale University Press, 1995.

Smith, Joseph Aubin. *Reminiscences of Saratoga*. New York: Knickerbocker Press, 1897.

St. Johns, Adela Rogers. *Final Verdict*. New York: Doubleday & Co., 1962.

Standiford, Les. *Last Train to Paradise: Henry Flagler and the Spectacular Rise and Fall of the Railroad That Crossed an Ocean*. New York: Broadway Books, 2002.

Sterngass, Jon. *First Resorts: Pursuing Pleasure at Saratoga Springs, Newport & Coney Island*. Baltimore: Johns Hopkins University Press, 2001.

Stiles, T. J. *The First Tycoon: The Epic Life of Cornelius Vanderbilt*. New York: Alfred A. Knopf, 2009.

Stilgoe, John R. *Metropolitan Corridor: Railroads and the American Scene*. New Haven, CT: Yale University Press, 1983.

Stone, Scott C. S. *Yesterday in Hawaii: A Voyage through Time*. Waipahu, HI: Island Heritage Publishing, 2003.

Thomas, Jerry. *How to Mix Drinks, or, The Bon-Vivant's Companion*. 1877. Reprint. Memphis, TN: General Books, 2012.

Thomas, Lately. *Delmonico's: A Century of Splendor*. Boston: Houghton Mifflin, 1967.

Tichi, Cecelia. *Civic Passions: Seven Who Launched Progressive America*. Chapel Hill: University of North Carolina Press, 2009.

——. *Jack London: A Writer's Fight for a Better America*. Chapel Hill: University of North Carolina Press, 2015.

———. *What Would Mrs. Astor Do? The Essential Guide to the Manners and Mores of the Gilded Age*. New York: New York University Press, 2017.

Twain, Mark. *Roughing It*. 1872. Reprint. New York: Book of the Month Club, 1992.

Vynne, Harold Richard. *The Woman That's Good: The Story of the Undoing of a Dreamer*. 1900. Reprint. Delhi: Pravana, n.d.

Warner, Nicholas O. *Spirits of America: Intoxication in Nineteenth-Century American Literature*. Norman: University of Oklahoma Press, 1997.

White, John R., Jr. *The American Railroad Passenger Car*. Baltimore: Johns Hopkins University Press, 1978.

Wondrich, David. *Imbibe!* New York: Perigee, 2015.

See also the New York Public Library Menu Collection at http://menus.nypl.org.

INDEX OF COCKTAIL RECIPES

ABOUT THE AUTHOR

A native of Chicago, the Steel City of the Gilded Age, Cecelia Tichi is an award-winning author and teacher whose half-dozen previous books survey the glittering manners and dubious mores of that era, its technology, and its movers and shakers from celebrated authors Jack London and Edith Wharton to steel mogul Andrew Carnegie. Cecelia teaches undergraduate and graduate courses in American literature and culture at Vanderbilt University. She lives in Nashville, Tennessee.